the

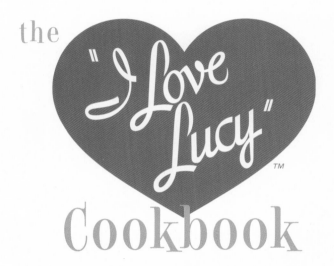

"I Love Lucy"™

Cookbook

the

"I Love Lucy"™

Cookbook

CLASSIC RECIPES INSPIRED
BY THE ICONIC TV SHOW

Jenn Fujikawa

RUNNING PRESS
PHILADELPHIA

RUNNING PRESS
Hachette Book Group
1290 Avenue of the Americas, New York, NY 10104
www.runningpress.com
@Running_Press

Printed in China
First Edition: December 2020

Published by Running Press, an imprint of Perseus Books, LLC, a subsidiary of Hachette Book Group, Inc. The Running Press name and logo is a trademark of the Hachette Book Group.

The Hachette Speakers Bureau provides a wide range of authors for speaking events. To find out more, go to www.hachettespeakersbureau.com or call (866) 376-6591.

The publisher is not responsible for websites (or their content) that are not owned by the publisher.

PHOTO CREDITS:
Food photos by Jenn Fujikawa except the following:
Shutterstock: pages v, vi, vii, 6, 10, 15, 17, 18, 21, 25, 33, 39, 42, 47, 54, 72, 83, 84, 89, 108, 109, 116, 125, 128, 132, 138, 139, 142, 145, 152, 153, 156, 171, and 173; Dreamstime: page 10; iStock: pages 16, 17, 33, 42, 47, 58, 90, 108, 109, 116, 128, 171, and 173; Alamy: pages v, 39; Paul Kepple: pages 54 and 153; 123RF: page 97.

Print book cover and interior design, spot illustrations, photo collages, and photo treatments by PAUL KEPPLE and ALEX BRUCE at HEADCASE DESIGN.
www.headcasedesign.com

Library of Congress Control Number: 2020942333
ISBNs: 978-0-7624-7180-5 (hardcover), 978-0-7624-7179-9 (ebook)
1010
10 9 8 7 6 5 4 3 2 1

CONTENTS

PART ONE

PART TWO

PART SIX

PART SEVEN

PART EIGHT

Introduction

SEVENTY YEARS AFTER its debut, *I Love Lucy* remains a television landmark, and Lucille Ball is an international icon and an inspiration to aspiring comedic performers. The show introduced the world to the wacky redhead who constantly gets herself into capers that keep her levelheaded bandleader husband, Ricky, on his toes. A pioneering tour de force of television history, the show's endurance is seen in myriad ways, including its easy availability on both the small screen, via DVD and streaming platforms, and the big screen, for special events. *I Love Lucy* remains truly beloved throughout the world.

Its characters are indelible. Along with Lucy and Ricky were their always-willing neighbors, Fred and Ethel Mertz. The foursome went on adventures that took them from their picturesque New York City apartments to the Swiss Alps, out to Hollywood, California, and more. On those trips they encountered both eclectic strangers and celebrities, all of whom somehow got roped into the Ricardo–Mertz shenanigans. For all the schemes they got into, they were incredibly relatable. These stars were "just like us." They laughed, they experienced big life moments together—and they ate . . . heartily and often.

Just think of some of the memorable scenes that revolved around eating and cooking. Always up for a scheme, selling Lucy's delicious recipe for her Aunt Martha's salad dressing seemed like the ideal way to make a quick buck. Along with Ethel, Lucy pitched the homemade concoction on television, and the viewer could practically taste the tangy dressing through the TV. The advertisement worked a little too well, as the gals found themselves overwhelmed with orders. On another adventure in a quaint winery in the Italian countryside, Lucy got earthy and tried out traditional wine-making by stomping grapes, only to have it result in an all-out brawl. Although the original episode was in black and white, the colors somehow seeped through the screen as grape stains appeared during the fight. And who can forget Lucy's tipsy TV pitch for a vitamin-filled, alcohol-laced "cure-all"? Vitameatavegamin may have been a made-up product, but its intoxicating pitch will be long remembered.

Dinners out were always a treat, making viewers privy to the hottest in mid-century restaurant menu fare. Still, cooking was a mainstay of the Ricardo home, and Lucy was in many ways the quintessential 1950s housewife. But she, of course, did it her own way. Whether she was making a roast for dinner or preparing a hearty breakfast, Lucy always had a way of bringing some humor into her cooking, making a day in the kitchen seem like a dream (and sometimes a nightmare!). We often got to see the Ricardos start their day off having breakfast together. It was usually a bounty of food, consisting of such morning staples as eggs and bacon, "flying" toast, fruit, and lots of coffee. For dinners, Lucy served up plenty of traditional American fare like roast beef and potatoes, as well as Cuban cuisine like Ricky's favorite meal, arroz con pollo.

Just as iconic as Lucy and Ricky were as a couple, so were Lucy and Ethel as best friends, with the two of them getting into some of the wackiest adventures as only two pals could—and more often than one would think, it involved food. None is more memorable than the hilarious comedy that ensued when Lucy and Ethel went to work at Kramer's Kandy Kitchen and were tasked with individually wrapping chocolates as they passed along a conveyor belt. Woefully outpaced, the two decided they had no choice but to hide the evidence of their failure by stuffing the sweets into their mouths and uniforms. In another memorable instance, the ladies agreed to their husbands' idea of going back to the turn of the century to keep house like their grandmothers, complete with butter-churning and old-fashioned home cooking. Only in the world of Lucy would she add more than four times the right amount of yeast to a recipe, resulting in the world's largest (and most delightful) loaf of bread.

While these show highlights have become iconic, there were also so many unsung scenes that involved food—like when Lucy and Ethel shared a car ride with a stranger (a possible hatchet murderess!) and choked down watercress sandwiches, or when Ricky put Lucy on a schedule, so she froze his morning coffee into a popsicle to show him an extreme means of time-saving. These unforgettable little foodie interludes, done in distinctly Lucy style, stick with us. Lucy's warmth and accessibility makes viewers feel like they're mixing into her adventures every step of the way, even cooking right along with her in the kitchen.

Part of the magic of the Ricardos and the Mertzes is their ability to draw us in. Maybe you've always wanted to pull up a chair at the table right alongside the fab four and enjoy a plate of arroz con pollo, or savor a sip of anniversary champagne, or have a sandwich with the ladies of the Wednesday Afternoon Fine Arts League. *The* I Love Lucy *Cookbook* brings you the next best thing: a collection of recipes featured in or inspired by the show. Each relates back to an episode, evoking visuals of Lucy making or eating the dish. While some recipes are undeniably 1950s classics, others are based on Ricky's favorite Cuban dishes

and the *I Love Lucy* episodes set in Europe, and you'll even find a tiny treat that's an ode to Little Ricky. Lucy and Ricky and Fred and Ethel's perennial friendship serves as the backdrop for the recipes in this book. The hope is that they motivate you to cook and spend time with the ones you love.

As you cook your way through these pages, remember that through it all Lucy always prevailed, and you can, too. Her biggest fails made for the biggest laughs, so have fun whipping up these dishes. These bountiful bites are ideally to be shared with friends and family, over joyful stories and maybe even a song or two. *Buen provecho!* (That's Spanish for happy feasting!)

PART ONE

A LITTLE BIT OF CUBA

THE BRILLIANCE OF Lucy and Ricky's dynamic is that despite their differences, they were the consummate couple. Ricky's roots in Cuba are key to not only his music, but to his personality. He often lost his temper over Lucy's antics and broke out into a diatribe of Spanish, but his love for her always shone through.

Ricky's joy when he sings of his homeland is palpable, and the recipes in this chapter relate to his native Cuba. Carne de Puerco con Chile Verde (page 8) is inspired by the episode "Lucy's Mother-in-Law." When Ricky's mother comes to visit, the first thing Lucy does is crack open a Cuban cookbook to see how she can make an impression with this classic Cuban dish. In the episode "Job Switching," Ricky himself decides to take on his favorite meal: arroz con pollo. He ends up with an explosion in the kitchen—a sloppy mess of rice from the floor to the ceiling. Don't worry, this chapter's recipe for Ricky's Favorite Arroz con Pollo on page 20 is much tidier, with authentic Cuban flavors that shine through like Ricky's love of his country.

In this chapter, enjoy this and many more dishes inspired by Cuba. Side note: Desi Arnaz was himself an extremely accomplished cook, known for making fabulous homemade Cuban cuisine for family and friends.

CUBAN MOJO CHICKEN

Inspired by Episode 8: "Men Are Messy" (Season 1)

◇◇

IN THIS CLASSIC episode, it's men vs. women in the battle of housekeeping, and the Ricardos' apartment gets divided in two. When Fred visits Ricky on "his side," Ricky offers him some leftover chicken, but the catch is—the kitchen is on Lucy's side of the apartment!

Inspired by Ricky's willingness to feed his pal, this classic Cuban chicken dish is marinated and roasted, and just as delicious no matter which side of the apartment it's served on.

MAKES 8 SERVINGS

1 whole chicken, cut into pieces

FOR THE MARINADE
⅓ cup olive oil
⅓ cup orange juice
¼ cup freshly squeezed lime juice

6 garlic cloves, minced
2 teaspoons cumin
2 teaspoons oregano
2 teaspoons salt
½ teaspoon freshly ground black pepper

• To make the marinade, in a small bowl, stir together the olive oil, orange juice, lime juice, garlic, cumin, oregano, salt, and pepper.
• Place the chicken in a sealable bag and pour in the marinade. Keep in the refrigerator for 6 hours or overnight.
• Preheat the oven to 375°F. Place the chicken in a roasting pan and discard the marinade.
• Bake for 1 hour or until an instant-read thermometer reads 165°F.
• Let rest for 5 minutes, then serve. Follow this dish with Aloha Cream Pie (page 124) and you'll have a scrumptious meal for visiting guests!

CARNE DE PUERCO CON CHILE VERDE

Inspired by Episode 105: "Lucy's Mother-in-Law" (Season 4)

◇◇

HAVING NEVER MET her mother-in-law, Lucy is anxious, and with Mother Ricardo's imminent arrival from Cuba, Lucy wants nothing more than to make a good impression. Cooking a quintessential Cuban dish is a surefire way to win her over, so Lucy consults a Cuban cookbook where she finds a recipe for Carne de Puerco con Chile Verde. Translated as "green chile pork stew," this dinner of simmering pork shoulder in salsa verde is a melt-in-your-mouth Cuban meal that no mother-in-law could possibly resist.

MAKES 4 TO 6 SERVINGS

FOR THE SALSA VERDE

1 pound tomatillos, husks removed, rinsed and dried

1 cup fresh cilantro, stems removed

1 cup diced onion

1 jalapeño, stemmed (seeded, if desired)

1 serrano pepper, stemmed (seeded, if desired)

4 garlic cloves

1 tablespoon freshly squeezed lime juice

½ teaspoon salt

FOR THE PORK

2 tablespoons olive oil

3 pounds pork butt, cubed

1 teaspoon salt

1 teaspoon freshly ground black pepper

• Preheat the oven to 400°F. Line a baking sheet with aluminum foil. Cut the tomatillos in half and place on the baking sheet. Roast for 15 to 20 minutes until almost falling apart. Let cool, until easy enough to handle.

• Place the roasted tomatillos in a blender. Add the cilantro, onion, jalapeño, serrano pepper, garlic, lime juice, and salt. Blend until combined. Set aside.

• In a Dutch oven over medium-high heat, brown the pork in the olive oil. Season with salt and pepper.

• Add the blended salsa verde. Cover and simmer on low for 1½ hours. Serve with rice, and your in-laws will welcome you with open arms.

BRING THE BULL IN THE RING AND LAUGH IN ITS FACE

Featured in Episode 92: "The Diner" (Season 3)

◇◇◇

RICKY IS READY to leave the entertainment business for steady work. Fred laments along with him, leading the Ricardos and Mertzes to join forces and open a diner. A terrible argument leads them to split the restaurant in two—literally right down the middle, with one half called "Little Bit of Cuba," and the other rechristened "Big Hunk of America." Emulating Fred's diner-speak, "Bring the bull in the ring and laugh in its face" is Ricky's version of an order for a hamburger with no onions. Inspired by this order, this juicy burger is made with a savory trio of beef, pork, and chorizo, topped with thin, fried shoestring potatoes and a touch of ketchup. Known colloquially as a frita, this uniquely Cuban burger is the perfect combination of the Caribbean and America, fitting easily on the menu of the gang's diner.

MAKES 6 SERVINGS

1 large russet potato	1 garlic clove, minced
Vegetable oil for frying	1 large egg
1 teaspoon salt, divided	1 teaspoon paprika
1 pound ground beef	½ teaspoon cumin
½ pound ground pork	¼ teaspoon freshly ground black pepper
½ pound chorizo	½ cup ketchup, for serving
1 cup dry breadcrumbs	6 buns
½ cup minced onion	

- Cut the potato into thin matchsticks. Place them in a large bowl of water for 45 minutes, then drain and dry thoroughly.
- In a Dutch oven, add the potatoes and pour in enough oil to just cover them. Turn the heat to medium high, until the oil starts to bubble. Cook for 30 minutes, until golden brown. Let drain, and immediately season with ½ teaspoon salt. Set aside.
- In a large bowl, combine the beef, pork, chorizo, breadcrumbs, onion, garlic, egg, paprika, cumin, the remaining salt, and pepper.
- Form the mixture into six patties and cook in a skillet over medium-high heat, until cooked through.
- Spread ketchup on the buns. Place a patty on the bottom bun, top with fried potatoes, then the top bun, to serve.
- This burger is both a little bit of Cuba and a big hunk of America, all in one bite!

BIG HUNK of AMERICA

CUBANO SANDWICH

Inspired by Episode 17: "Lucy Writes a Play" (Season 1)

LUCY DECIDES TO write a play that's "dripping with drama, dripping with intrigue, dripping with excitement," and its setting is Havana. When Ricky refuses to participate in the production, Lucy changes the locale, but the lure of a Caribbean island can't be beat—and neither can this sandwich. This classic Cubano is a heavenly blend of ham, roasted pork, cheese, and pickles on delicious pan-pressed Cuban bread. A taste combination so beautiful, it's simply inspirational for all creative endeavors!

MAKES 2 SERVINGS

FOR THE PORK
3 pound pork shoulder
Mojo marinade (page 7)

FOR THE SANDWICHES
2 Cuban *bolillo* (bread rolls)
3 tablespoons yellow mustard

6 slices ham
6 slices roast pork
6 slices Swiss cheese
1 dill pickle, cut into slices lengthwise
2 tablespoons unsalted butter

- Place the pork in a sealable bag and pour in the marinade. Keep in the refrigerator for 6 hours or overnight.
- Preheat the oven to 325°F.
- Cook the roast for 1¹⁄₂ hours or until an internal thermometer reads 145°F. Remove from the oven and cover with aluminum foil. Let rest for 15 minutes. Cut into thin slices.
- Slice the bread in half and generously spread the mustard on both sides. To assemble each sandwich, layer the ham, roast pork, cheese, and pickles between the two slices of bread.
- Melt the butter in a skillet over medium-high heat, add a sandwich, and place a heavy cast iron skillet on top, pressing down onto the bread.
- Cook until golden brown, then turn the sandwich over and repeat with the skillet press, until the cheese is melted.
- Slice in half to serve, and let this tasty treat inspire your creativity!

Cooking Cuban Style

Ricky's Cuban roots are a recurring theme in *I Love Lucy*, whether it's his transition between Spanish and English in conversation, or the Latin music he performs at the club. The show highlights the cultural differences between Lucy and Ricky, but it also illustrates how Ricky's background makes them stronger and adds considerable pizzazz to their union (especially in contrast to the Mertzes!).

By mentioning his favorite meal of arroz con pollo throughout the series, Ricky introduced 1950s audiences to something that sounds exotic, but when you break it down it's a dish that's universal: chicken and rice. Every culture has its own version of this protein and side, but no matter how it's prepared, it's pure comfort food.

Ever supportive, throughout the series Lucy often finds ways to give Ricky a touch or taste of his homeland. Whether it's fixing up the house into a Havana-wonderland with classic party food, or studying a Cuban cookbook to impress her mother-in-law, Lucy is always all-in—and sometimes overboard—when it comes to bringing the lifestyle and traditions of Cuba into their home.

"I'm on my way to Cuba, that's where I'm going.... Cuba, that's where I'll stay."

—RICKY, IN THE SONG "I'LL SEE YOU IN C-U-B-A"

PASTELITOS DE GUAYABA

Inspired by Episode 28: "Cuban Pals" (Season 1)

◇◇

RICKY'S OLD FRIENDS from Cuba come to visit and although there's a bit of a language barrier, that won't stop Lucy from being the consummate hostess. The best way to entertain company is with refreshments, so Lucy arranges a beautiful tray of appetizers to make her guests feel at home. Inspired by her cordiality, these *pastelitos* are Cuban pastries stuffed with sweet guava filling. They're always a crowd-pleaser and a great way to break the ice among new friends!

MAKES 12 SERVINGS

1 package (17 ounces) puff pastry, thawed	4 tablespoons guava jelly
1 bar (14 ounces) guava paste	1 large egg mixed with 1 tablespoon water, for egg wash

- Preheat the oven to 400°F. Prep a baking sheet with Silpats or parchment paper.
- Place 1 sheet of puff pastry on the baking sheet.
- Cut the guava paste into 12 thin slices and place them on the puff pastry. Add a teaspoon of guava jelly on top of each slice.
- Place the second sheet of puff pastry on top. Cut into 12 pieces. Score the top of each piece, and brush with the egg wash.
- Bake for 20 minutes, until golden brown. Let cool on a wire rack.
- Once cooled, serve and you'll make instant friends!

RICKY'S FAVORITE ARROZ CON POLLO

Featured in Episode 39: "Job Switching" (Season 2)

◇◇

YOU CAN TAKE the boy out of Cuba but you can't take Cuba out of the boy. Whenever Ricky gets a hankering for a taste of home, he makes mention of his favorite meal, arroz con pollo. It may be a simple aromatic dish of simmered chicken and rice, but when Ricky endeavors to make it himself, let's just say it doesn't go as planned. By turning up the pressure cooker and also adding too much rice to the pot, Ricky and Fred end up in a physical battle with flying chickens and exploding rice, with only a dustpan and broom to defend themselves. This recipe takes a much calmer approach to cooking and is a hearty and delicious version of Ricky's favorite dinner.

MAKES 4 SERVINGS

FOR THE CHICKEN
6 bone-in chicken thighs
1 teaspoon salt
½ teaspoon cumin
¼ teaspoon pepper
2 tablespoons vegetable oil

FOR THE RICE
2 tablespoons olive oil
1 onion, diced
1 red bell pepper, seeded and diced

4 garlic cloves, minced
2 cups long-grain rice
2 cups chicken stock
1 can (14 ounces) diced tomatoes
2 teaspoons cumin
1 teaspoon annatto powder
1 teaspoon oregano
½ teaspoon salt
¼ teaspoon freshly ground black pepper
1 bay leaf
½ cup frozen peas

• Season the chicken thighs with salt, cumin, and pepper.
• Heat the oil in a Dutch oven over medium-high heat and place the chicken thighs in the pot to brown on all sides. Remove and set aside.
• To the same pot, add the onion, red bell pepper, and garlic. Cook until softened.
• Add the rice, chicken stock, tomatoes, cumin, annatto powder, oregano, salt, pepper, and bay leaf. Bring to a boil.
• Reduce the heat and nestle the chicken into the rice. Cover and simmer on low for 45 minutes.
• Fluff the rice, then add the peas. Cover and cook for another 10 minutes. Let cool slightly, then serve up for a mouthwatering taste of Cuba!

Rinse chicken before cooking, but please, don't use cleanser!

EASY ON THE RICE!
Use half cup per person— never more—else it may end up on the kitchen floor!

RICKY:
"Hey listen, by the way, what do you know about rice?"

FRED:
"Well, I had it thrown at me on one of the darkest days of my life."

FIESTA EMPANADAS

Inspired by Episode 2: "Be a Pal" (Season 1)

◇◇

LUCY THINKS RICKY is homesick, so she turns the apartment into a mini-Havana to remind him of his childhood in Cuba. She puts on a show, complete with a fiesta full of food, fun, and even live chickens.

Whether in Cuba or a New York City apartment, Lucy would surely be serving up these savory turnovers filled with succulent meat. For your next fiesta, try this easy-to-prepare recipe that's sure to be a hit!

MAKES 36 EMPANADAS

FOR THE DOUGH
3 cups all-purpose flour
½ cup (1 stick) cold unsalted butter, cut into cubes
½ teaspoon salt
1 large egg
½ cup whole milk

FOR THE FILLING
1 tablespoon olive oil
1 onion, minced
1 green bell pepper, seeded and minced
2 garlic cloves, minced
1 pound ground beef

1 teaspoon cumin
½ teaspoon oregano
½ teaspoon salt
¼ teaspoon freshly ground black pepper
1 bay leaf
½ cup tomato sauce
3 tablespoons dry sherry
2 teaspoons Worcestershire sauce
½ cup pimiento-stuffed green olives, minced
¼ cup raisins

FOR THE ASSEMBLY
1 large egg mixed with 1 tablespoon water, for egg wash

• In a large bowl, use a pastry cutter to mix together the flour, butter, salt, and egg. Add the milk, a little at a time, until the dough comes together. Wrap in plastic wrap and chill in the refrigerator until ready to use.

• In a skillet over medium-high heat, add the olive oil and cook the onion, bell pepper, and garlic, until softened.

• Add the ground beef and cook until browned.

• Stir in the cumin, oregano, salt, pepper, and bay leaf. Pour in the tomato sauce, sherry, and Worcestershire sauce. Stir in the olives and raisins. Simmer on low for 10 minutes. Let cool.

• Preheat the oven to 400°F. Prep baking sheets with Silpats or parchment paper.

- On a floured surface, roll the dough out to ⅛ inch thick. Use a 6-inch round cutter to cut out circles.
- Place two tablespoons of filling in the center of each pastry circle and brush the edges with the egg wash.
- Bring the edges together, pinching to close. Starting at the right corner, pinch and fold to create a fluted edge. Brush with the egg wash. Space the empanadas about 2 inches apart on the baking sheet.
- Bake for 15 to 18 minutes, until golden brown.

ROPA VIEJA

Inspired by Episode 162: "The Ricardos Visit Cuba" (Season 6)

◇◇

MEETING IN-LAWS IS always nerve-wracking, but having your first encounter be in an entirely new country can make it downright scary. While we know Lucy can charm anyone, Ricky's Uncle Alberto is a hard nut to crack. After crushing Alberto's prized cigars, Lucy ventures out to repair her mess, but finds herself hiding out in the factory, even stuffing the tobacco in the cigars herself. Eventually Uncle Alberto and Lucy bond over their mutual love for Little Ricky and all is forgotten.

Instead of cigars, Lucy should also have turned to the universal equalizer: food. Cuban specialties are an excellent way to break down language barriers. A braised beef entreé whose name literally translates to "old clothes," ropa vieja is the national dish of Cuba, and it tastes much better than its name!

MAKES 6 SERVINGS

2 pounds beef flank steak	1 teaspoon paprika
3 teaspoons cumin, divided	1 can (15 ounces) crushed tomatoes
2 teaspoons salt, divided	1 cup beef broth
1¼ teaspoons freshly ground black pepper, divided	½ cup white wine
1 tablespoon vegetable oil	1 can (6 ounces) tomato paste
1 onion, thinly sliced	1 tablespoon white vinegar
1 red bell pepper, seeded and thinly sliced	1 bay leaf
6 garlic cloves, minced	1 cup pimiento-stuffed olives
1 teaspoon oregano	¼ cup capers
	2 tablespoons cilantro, chopped

• Season the beef with 1 teaspoon each of cumin, salt, and pepper.

• Add the oil to a Dutch oven. Over medium-high heat, brown the beef on all sides. Remove and set aside.

• Add the onion, bell pepper, and garlic. Cook until softened.

• Stir in the remaining cumin, salt, and pepper, and the oregano, paprika, tomatoes, beef broth, wine, tomato paste, vinegar, and bay leaf. Bring to a boil.

• Add the beef back to the pot, cover, and simmer on low for 2 hours.

• Remove the meat and shred it with two forks.

• Return the meat to the pot and stir in the pimiento olives and capers. Cook for 30 minutes.

• Stir in the cilantro. When served with rice and beans, this meal is sure to win over any family member!

RICKY:

"What did you say?"

LUCY:

"He asked me if I wanted some punch.
I said, *si, macho grasa.*"

RICKY:

"*Macho grasa?* Oh, dear, it's *muchas gracias.*
You just called him a big, fat pig."

PART TWO

A BIG HUNK
OF AMERICA

NINETEEN FIFTIES AMERICAN dinners were unique and undeniably hearty. Meat and potatoes were the standard fare, and Lucy's dinner-planning often included a roasted item, whether it be beef, chicken, or lamb. While meat took center stage, the multitude of side dishes that accompanied the meal were sometimes just as robust as the main dish itself. Whether salads, gelatins, or soups, the courses were varied and filling. (Speaking of salad, in this chapter you'll finally be able to taste for yourself Lucy's Aunt Martha's Old-Fashioned Salad Dressing from the "Million-Dollar Idea" episode!)

Lucy typically cooked at home, but her dining-out ventures often brought about memorable scenes as well. While Lucy, Ethel, and Fred were in Los Angeles, they stopped for lunch at the Brown Derby, a known celebrity hot spot. It was here that an encounter with actor Bill Holden was undone, thanks to a mouthful of the restaurant's famous spaghetti. Now you can make your own version of this classic pasta dish, without any celebrity distractions.

This chapter of American classics relives the standard dishes that were once the centerpiece of family dinner tables in the '50s. One taste and you'll instantly be whisked back to mid-century modern America.

THICK AND JUICY LAMB CHOPS

Featured in Episode 49: "Lucy Changes Her Mind" (Season 2)

◇◇◇

THERE'S NOTHING WRONG with changing your mind once. Twice? Third time's the charm. Lucy is indecisive, but who can blame her when it comes to ordering from an elegant restaurant menu? Out for dinner, Lucy soundly makes a decision and requests roast beef, but her firm resolve wavers upon hearing Ricky's order of sirloin steak and Fred's desire for pork chops. But it's Ethel's choice of lamb chops that initially makes Lucy decide that she simply must change her order. One taste of these succulent chops and you'll know you made the right decision. After all, you don't want to have dinner regrets.

MAKES 4 SERVINGS

3 tablespoons olive oil, divided

1 teaspoon rosemary

1¼ teaspoons salt, divided

½ teaspoon freshly ground black pepper, divided

4 thick lamb chops, trimmed of fat

2 tablespoons unsalted butter, divided

1 shallot, minced

1 cup white wine

2 tablespoons heavy whipping cream

• In a small bowl, mix together 1½ tablespoons olive oil, the rosemary, 1 teaspoon salt, and ¼ teaspoon pepper. Rub onto the lamb chops and set aside.

• In a skillet over medium-high heat, add the remaining olive oil and 1 tablespoon of butter. Sear the lamb chops until browned.

• Flip, and cook for 4 to 5 minutes, to an internal temperature of 125°F. Remove the chops from the pan and cover with foil to keep warm.

• Add the shallot to the pan drippings and cook until soft. Whisk in the wine, and cook until the liquid is reduced by half. Turn off the heat. Stir in the remaining tablespoon of butter and the cream, until thickened. Season with remaining salt and pepper.

• Pour the sauce over the chops to serve. Once you decide to make these, you won't regret your decision!

AUNT MARTHA'S OLD-FASHIONED SALAD DRESSING

Featured in Episode 79: "The Million-Dollar Idea" (Season 3)

LUCY'S OLD FAMILY recipe for salad dressing is so tasty, the gals decide to go into business selling it. The plan proves to be successful . . . too successful, and Lucy and Ethel become overwhelmed with orders. To try to get out of the business, they create a TV spot in which Lucy's toothless alter ego tries to convince the world that it tastes awful. Her act backfires when the viewing public thinks it's all a joke, and they start clamoring for even more of Aunt Martha's old-fashioned salad dressing! Even without Lucy and Ethel's promotion, this recipe's tempting taste will make it an instant classic in your home.

MAKES 12 SERVINGS

¼ cup minced sweet onion
¼ cup white vinegar
2 tablespoons honey
2 teaspoons Dijon mustard

1 teaspoon freshly squeezed lemon juice
½ teaspoon celery seed
¼ teaspoon salt
¾ cup vegetable oil

- Place the onion, vinegar, honey, Dijon mustard, lemon juice, celery seed, and salt in a blender.
- As it blends, pour in a steady stream of oil until the dressing comes together.
- Keep in the refrigerator in an airtight container until ready to use. This dressing is so good you'll want to drink it straight out of the container.

"For years, only a few close friends and
relatives knew the thrill of eating salad
made with Aunt Martha's Old-Fashioned Salad
Dressing, but Aunt Martha—sweet, lovable,
kind old lady that she is—has finally
consented to let the world in on her secret."

—ETHEL

Aunt Martha's

Old Fashioned

Salad Dressing

DUCK BREAST WITH A RED WINE SAUCE

Inspired by Episode 64: "The Camping Trip" (Season 2)

◇◇

ON A CAMPING trip, Lucy tries to prove to Ricky that a weekend outdoors is just what the couple needs to grow closer. Despite the fact that ducks live in water, Lucy managed to go hunting and shoot a duck out of a tree—fully cleaned and plucked, thanks to a helpful Ethel, of course. If you should be so lucky as to happen upon a dinner-ready duck, try this recipe for serving it with a rich, flavorful wine sauce.

MAKES 4 SERVINGS

FOR THE DUCK

4 boneless, skin-on duck breasts

2 teaspoons salt

1 teaspoon freshly ground black pepper

2 tablespoons olive oil

FOR THE SAUCE

2 tablespoons unsalted butter, divided

1 shallot, minced

1 garlic clove, minced

2 sprigs fresh rosemary

1 cup chicken stock

⅓ cup red wine

2 tablespoons orange juice

• Lightly score the duck skin in a diamond-shaped pattern. Season with salt and pepper.

• In a skillet over medium-high heat, add the olive oil and sear the duck breasts skin-side down until browned. Turn the duck over and cook for another 5 minutes, to an internal temperature of 170°F. Remove the duck from the heat and let rest for 10 minutes.

• In the pan with the drippings, over medium heat, add 1 tablespoon butter and the shallot, garlic, and rosemary.

• Whisk in the chicken stock, wine, and orange juice. Simmer until the liquid reduces by half, 8 to 10 minutes.

• Strain the sauce into a small bowl, and stir in the remaining tablespoon of butter.

• Slice the duck and serve with sauce, no hunting gear necessary!

STUFFED PORK CHOPS

Featured in Episode 33: "Lucy's Schedule" (Season 1)

◇◇

BEING PUNCTUAL ISN'T always easy, but when Ricky puts Lucy on a schedule, timing is everything. Late again, the Ricardos show up for dinner at the home of Ricky's new boss, Mr. Littlefield, having just missed the meal. Lucy laments not being able to taste Mrs. Littlefield's thick, stuffed pork chops, resulting in rumbling tummies and a desperate move for a piece of waxed fruit. Don't let that happen to you! Now you can cook up your own chops, and it won't even throw you off your timetable.

MAKES 4 SERVINGS

4 (1-inch-thick) bone-in pork chops	½ teaspoon thyme
1 tablespoon unsalted butter	½ teaspoon marjoram
½ cup diced onion	½ teaspoon sage
1 celery rib, diced	1 tablespoon olive oil
1 garlic clove, minced	¼ teaspoon salt
8 ounces dry bread cubes	¼ teaspoon freshly ground
½ cup chicken stock	black pepper
1 teaspoon chopped parsley	

• Preheat the oven to 375°F.
• Cut a slit down the side of each chop, until it almost reaches the bone.
• In a skillet over medium-high heat, add the butter, onion, celery, and garlic. Cook until softened.
• In a large bowl, stir together the bread cubes, chicken stock, onion mixture, parsley, thyme, marjoram, and sage.
• Spoon the stuffing into the pockets of the chops, and place in a baking dish. Drizzle the chops with olive oil and season with salt and pepper.
• Bake for 30 minutes, or until an instant-read thermometer reads 145°F. Serve this with a side salad topped with Aunt Martha's Old-Fashioned Salad Dressing (page 31), which you can make a day ahead so you'll stay on schedule!

HAPPY LITTLE LOAF
OF BREAD

Featured in Episode 25: "Pioneer Women" (Season 1)

◇◇

THE MODERN CONVENIENCES of 1952 make housework too easy, or so Ricky and Fred think. So they bet that the gals can't live life like their grandmothers did at the turn of the century—that means churning butter and baking bread. When preparing her bread dough, Lucy adds too much yeast, and the result is a massive loaf that sends her clear across the kitchen when she opens the oven door. Not to worry, this recipe has just the right amount of leavening, and will result in a perfect pioneer loaf.

MAKES 10 SERVINGS

1½ cups warm water (110°F)

2 teaspoons granulated sugar

1 packet (2¼ teaspoons) yeast

2 tablespoons honey

1 teaspoon salt

3¼ cups all-purpose flour

¼ cup (½ stick) unsalted butter, melted

Olive oil, for greasing

• In the bowl of an electric mixer fitted with a dough hook, add the warm water, sugar, and yeast. Let the mixture sit for 5 minutes, until bubbly.

• Stir in the honey and salt. Add the flour, 1 cup at a time, until the dough forms a ball.

• Turn out the dough onto a floured surface, and knead for 5 minutes.

• Grease a large bowl and a loaf pan with olive oil. Place the dough inside the bowl, cover the bowl with a clean kitchen towel, and let rise until the dough doubles in size, approximately 2 hours.

• Punch down the dough, then place in the greased loaf pan. Cover and let rise for another hour.

• Preheat the oven to 375°F. Bake for 25 to 30 minutes, until the internal temperature is 190°F.

• Remove from oven and brush with the melted butter. Let cool completely.

• Slice the bread, share with friends, and dive right in. There's nothing better than homemade bread with home-churned butter!

"Listen, your grandmothers didn't have any of these modern electrical conveniences, and they not only washed the dishes but they swept the floor, they churned the butter, they baked the bread, they did the laundry, and they made their own clothes . . ."

LUCY:

"Sure, where are those women today? Dead."

FRAGRANT ROAST BEEF

Featured in Episode 29: "The Freezer" (Season 1)

◇◇

ALWAYS TRYING TO save money, Lucy and Ethel buy a used walk-in freezer from Ethel's uncle. The deal seems like a money-saver, especially when you can buy meat at wholesale prices. A side of beef doesn't sound like much, so Lucy orders two, resulting in an endless delivery of over 700 pounds of beef. To hide her mistake, she places the beef in the furnace, culminating in the world's biggest barbeque. Soon the entire apartment building is filled with the fragrant smell of roasting meat. Now you can bring that delectable aroma into your own home with this flavorful, aromatic roast beef.

"Don't ask questions, just get a knife and a fork and a bottle of ketchup and follow me to the biggest barbecue in the whole world."

—LUCY

MAKES 6 SERVINGS

3 pounds top round roast, at room temperature	2 teaspoons rosemary
4 garlic cloves, sliced	2 teaspoons thyme
2 tablespoons olive oil	2 teaspoons salt
2 teaspoons oregano	1 teaspoon freshly ground black pepper

• Preheat the oven to 375°F. Make small cuts in the beef and insert the garlic slices. Rub the roast with olive oil.

• In a small bowl, combine the oregano, rosemary, thyme, salt, and pepper. Rub onto the roast.

• Place the meat on a rack in a roasting pan and cook for 15 minutes.

• Reduce the heat to 300°F and cook for another 45 minutes, or until a meat thermometer reads 135°F.

• Remove the roast from the oven and tent with foil. Let rest for 20 minutes.

• Slice to serve. If you were living in 1951, you, too, might be tempted to buy a side or two of beef at a mere 79 cents a pound! Enjoy this fragrant roast beef with a side of Gratin Dauphinois (page 62).

WARNING!
Never take the key into the freezer with you!

DELICIOUS ROAST CHICKEN

Featured in Episode 157: "Little Ricky Learns to Play the Drums" (Season 6)

◇◇

WHEN YOUR CHILD shows percussion prowess, it's best not to discourage him, even if the constant beat of the drums might drive you crazy. Still, Little Ricky's musical aspirations won't damper Lucy's need to cook a good dinner. When Ricky comes home, Lucy prepares him a delicious roast chicken, or at least she tries to. It turns out Fred's retaliation against the drumming noise was to turn off the Ricardos' electricity, leaving Lucy with an oven full of raw chicken. Sans those interruptions, this recipe should yield you a terrific-tasting chicken that will have your mouth moving to the beat.

MAKES 8 SERVINGS

3 tablespoons unsalted butter, at room temperature

1 tablespoon salt

2 teaspoons rosemary

1 teaspoon freshly ground black pepper

6 to 8 garlic cloves, smashed

1 (3- to 4-pound) whole chicken, neck and giblets discarded

1 lemon, halved

• Preheat the oven to 425°F.

• In a small bowl, combine the butter, salt, rosemary, pepper, and garlic. Rub the mixture both on the outside of the chicken and inside its cavity. Place the lemon halves inside as well.

• Tie the legs of the chicken together with kitchen twine and tuck the wings under. Place the chicken on a rack in a roasting pan.

• Roast for 1½ hours, or until an instant-read thermometer reads 165°F.

• Tent with foil and let rest for 15 minutes. Slice to serve. This roast chicken is the ideal meal for keeping your spirits up through your family's most challenging new hobbies.

BROWN DERBY– INSPIRED SPAGHETTI AND MEATBALLS

Featured in Episode 114: "L.A. at Last" (Season 4)

◇◇

LUCY'S LUNCH AT the Brown Derby brings her up close and personal with Hollywood heartthrob William Holden. Turning the tables, he gawks in her direction, resulting in the spaghetti taking center stage when Lucy gets stuck with a mouthful. It's Ethel to the rescue, as she resourcefully pulls a pair of tiny scissors from her purse to trim the unwieldy pasta.

As much as the Brown Derby was a celebrated haven for Hollywood luminaries, the fabled restaurant was also known for its inventive menu. Having created the first Cobb salad, the establishment also featured menu staples like savory seafood, Mexican favorites, and this full-flavored spaghetti meat sauce.

FOR THE MEATBALLS
½ pound ground beef
½ pound ground pork
1 garlic clove, minced
1 cup dry breadcrumbs
⅓ cup Parmesan cheese
1½ tablespoons chopped parsley
1 large egg
¼ cup whole milk
1 tablespoon olive oil

FOR THE MEAT SAUCE
2 tablespoons olive oil
1 onion, diced
2 garlic cloves, minced
1 pound ground beef
½ pound ground pork

½ pound ground veal
2 cups sliced mushrooms
2 tablespoons dried mushrooms
2 cups beef stock
1 cup Burgundy wine
1 (28-ounce) can crushed tomatoes
1 (15-ounce) can tomato sauce
1½ tablespoons salt
2 teaspoons freshly ground black pepper
1½ teaspoons paprika
½ teaspoon basil
½ teaspoon oregano
¼ teaspoon nutmeg
¼ teaspoon rosemary
½ bay leaf
1 (16-ounce) package spaghetti

• In a large bowl, combine the ground beef, ground pork, garlic, breadcrumbs, Parmesan cheese, parsley, egg, and milk. Form 16 meatballs.

• In a skillet over medium-high heat, add the olive oil and brown the meatballs in batches on all sides. Set aside.

• In a Dutch oven over medium-high heat, add the olive oil and sauté the onion and garlic until soft. Add the ground beef, ground pork, and ground veal, and cook until browned. Skim off the grease. Stir in the mushrooms and dried mushrooms. Cook for 2 to 3 minutes. Pour in the beef stock, wine, tomatoes, and tomato sauce. Stir in the salt, pepper, paprika, basil, oregano, nutmeg, rosemary, and bay leaf. Simmer on low for 45 minutes.

• Place the meatballs in the sauce and simmer for another 45 minutes. Skim off any grease on the surface as needed with a large spoon, and discard.

• Cook the spaghetti according to package instructions. Serve with meatballs and sauce. Pull up a chair alongside a dreamy dinner companion and feel free to gaze into their eyes between bites.

LUCY:

"Well, I suppose we could just drive up and down the streets and hunt movie stars. Tracking them down one by one takes so much time. I wonder if there's any place where they get together in a big herd?"

FRED:

"Well, maybe at sundown they all gather at the same watering hole."

LUCY:

"That's it! That's where we'll go!"

ETHEL:

"Where?"

LUCY:

"The watering hole! Fellow hunters, we're going to the Brown Derby!"

PART THREE

EUROPEAN DELIGHTS

IN SEASON 5, Ricky's band gets booked in Europe, which opens up a whole new world of travel and excitement for the Ricardos and Mertzes. From London to Scotland, Paris to Switzerland, and finally, Italy, all these exotic locales proved that Lucy could live life—and eat—to the fullest no matter where she was in the world.

The recipes in this chapter highlight the stops on the Ricardos' overseas vacation. In "Lucy Goes to Scotland," a whimsical dream featured Lucy's McGillicuddy ancestors, and led to Scottish-inspired recipes like traditional cock-a-leekie soup and Scottish stew, renamed here McGillicuddy Soup (page 73) and Dragon's Dinner Beef Stew (page 68). In "Paris at Last," Lucy's lack of knowledge of the French language caused her to order Escargots de Bourgogne (page 59). Playing a classic American stereotype, the only way she could stomach a plate of snails was to ask for a douse of ketchup—a no-no in any French bistro. You'll get the recipe here, no translation necessary.

But Lucy shone brightest in the episode "Lucy's Italian Movie." With Italy as her backdrop, her unforgettable jaunt in a winery vat ended in a skirmish for the ages. The smashed grapes scene inspired the recipe for Bitter Grapes Sangria on page 55, and it doesn't even require you to take off your shoes.

With their aromatic flavors and unique ingredients, these European Delights will take you along on Lucy's 1950s European holiday.

BITTER GRAPES SANGRIA

Inspired by Episode 150: "Lucy's Italian Movie" (Season 5)

◇◇

LUCY'S ROMP IN Italy is where she prepares for a role of a lifetime in a movie called *Bitter Grapes* by famed Italian producer Vittorio Philippi. To get into character and "soak up some local color," she goes to the Italian countryside and gets into a vat of trouble stomping grapes at a traditional winery. Who knew grape-stomping was a competitive sport? Keep yourself dry and free of wine stains with this sangria that's reminiscent of the flavorful fruits Lucy's labor may have produced. Once in your glass, it's vigorously smashed and ready to be sipped, all while you dream of la dolce vita.

MAKES 6 SERVINGS

1 cup red grapes	¼ cup freshly squeezed lemon juice
3 tablespoons light brown sugar	1 bottle red wine
1 cup orange juice	1 cup frozen red grapes
⅓ cup spiced rum	1 cup ice, plus more for serving

• Place the grapes and sugar in a large pitcher and muddle lightly. Stir in the orange juice, rum, and lemon juice.

• Pour in the red wine, frozen grapes, and ice. Place in the refrigerator until ready to serve.

• Serve over ice, and remember, life's too short to get into a grape-stomping grudge match.

LUCY:

"Gee, did you hear that, honey? It's going to be called *Bitter Grapes.* I wonder what part they want me for."

FRED:

"Oh, you're probably going to be one of the bunch."

ESCARGOTS DE BOURGOGNE

Featured in Episode 145: "Paris at Last" (Season 5)

◇◇

ANOTHER LANGUAGE BARRIER spells trouble for Lucy—this time it's not Spanish but French—when she finds herself dining alone in Paris. Unaware of what she's getting herself into, Lucy energetically orders escargot. Snails may be a delicacy in France, but are far from conventional to this redheaded American. Still, anything swimming in butter and garlic can't be all that bad. Just be sure to avoid Lucy's very American faux pas of dousing your dish in ketchup.

MAKES 4 SERVINGS

½ cup (1 stick) unsalted butter, at room temperature

2 garlic cloves, minced

2 teaspoons fresh parsley, minced

½ teaspoon salt

¼ teaspoon freshly ground black pepper

1 tablespoon olive oil

1 can (7 ounces) snails, rinsed and dried

1 tablespoon minced shallot

2 tablespoons white wine

2 tablespoons lemon juice

12 large snail shells

Sliced baguette, for serving

• In a small bowl, stir together the butter, garlic, parsley, salt, and pepper. Set aside.

• In a skillet over medium-high heat, add the olive oil, snails, and shallot. Cook for 1 to 2 minutes, then add the wine and lemon juice. Sauté until softened, 10 minutes.

• Drain the liquid and place a snail in each shell, followed by a generous spoonful of the butter mixture.

• Place in a baking dish and broil for 2 to 3 minutes.

• Serve with bread, but take manners into account; don't follow Lucy's lead and embarrass your dining companions by clamping your nose with the snail tongs.

"I think an
American
cousin
of yours
ate my
geranium
plant."

—LUCY

GRATIN DAUPHINOIS

Inspired by Episode 147: "Lucy Gets a Paris Gown" (Season 5)

◇◇

THE BISTROS ON the streets of Paris have some of the most delectable French dishes, and dining alfresco provides views of all the latest fashions as they cat-walk right before your eyes. After a Paris fashion show, Lucy dreams of owning a runway dress of her own and goes on a hunger strike to get her way. Even though she hides food throughout the apartment to sustain her, these inspired layered potatoes surely would have caused her to cave. When choosing between a designer dress or eating well, these deliciously creamy potatoes are the right choice.

MAKES 6 TO 8 SERVINGS

2 tablespoons unsalted butter, at room temperature

6 russet potatoes, peeled and cut into ⅛-inch-thick slices

4 cups whole milk

1 garlic clove, smashed

1½ teaspoons salt

½ teaspoon freshly ground black pepper

¼ teaspoon nutmeg

2 cups heavy whipping cream

2 cups grated Gruyère cheese

• Grease a 13- x 9-inch baking dish with butter.

• In a Dutch oven over medium-high heat, bring the potatoes, milk, and garlic to a simmer for 8 to 10 minutes, until the potatoes have softened but are not falling apart.

• Preheat the oven to 350°F.

• Layer the potatoes in the prepped baking dish. Season with salt, pepper, and nutmeg. Pour the heavy whipping cream over them, and evenly spread the cheese on top. Bake for 30 minutes.

• Let stand for 5 minutes, then serve. You may have to size up in your designer dress after you eat these potatoes, but it's worth it!

SWISS CHEESE SANDWICH

Featured in Episode 148: "Lucy in the Swiss Alps" (Season 5)

◇◇

HIKING IN THE Swiss Alps isn't for the weak, especially when a snowstorm hits. The Ricardos and Mertzes end up stranded on the mountain with nothing but cheese sandwiches in their backpacks. While Ricky, Fred, and Ethel all eat their rations, only Lucy is smart enough to save some of her sandwich for later. Inspired by the *Lucy* gang's ordeal and savory snack, this grilled grinder is made with melty Swiss cheese, balanced with crisp apple slices, buttered and toasted, and ready for a wintry hike. Just be sure to check the weather forecast before you head out!

MAKES 1 SANDWICH

1 tablespoon unsalted butter, at room temperature	4 slices Swiss cheese
2 slices sourdough bread	½ Granny Smith apple, thinly sliced

• Spread half the butter on one slice of bread.

• In a skillet over medium-high heat, place the bread buttered-side down. Top with two slices of cheese, apple, and two more slices of cheese.

• Place the second slice of bread on top, and spread the rest of the butter evenly on top.

• When the bottom bread is toasted, flip the sandwich and cook until the cheese is melted and the second bread slice is browned.

• Remove from the pan and slice in half to serve. You don't need to be stranded on a mountaintop to enjoy this scrumptious sandwich.

MUSHROOM AND SAUSAGE PIZZA

Featured in Episode 158: "Visitor from Italy" (Season 6)

◇◇

WHEN MARIO—A GONDOLIER they met on their trip to Italy—stops in for a visit, the Ricardos are puzzled. They quickly realize that he's mistakenly landed in New York to visit his brother, who actually lives in San Francisco, on the other side of the country. Refusing their money to fund his trip to the West Coast to find his brother, Mario gets a job as a pizza maker in hopes of earning his own passage. The trouble is, traveling with a visitor's visa, he's not actually allowed to work in the States legally, so it's Lucy to the rescue. She can take on any challenge, even one that requires graceful dough acrobatics. Watching her pizza prep is a magical flour-filled ballet, one that will make you hungry for your own pizza pie.

FOR THE DOUGH

¾ cup warm water (110°F)

1 packet (2¼ teaspoons) instant yeast

1 teaspoon granulated sugar

2 tablespoons olive oil, plus more for greasing

1 teaspoon salt

2½ cups all-purpose flour

FOR THE TOPPINGS

½ cup pizza sauce

2½ cups shredded mozzarella cheese, divided

1 cup Italian sausage

½ cup sliced fresh mushrooms

1 teaspoon oregano

½ teaspoon basil

• In the bowl of an electric mixer fitted with a dough hook, add the warm water, yeast, and sugar. Let sit for 5 minutes, until bubbly.

• Stir in the olive oil and salt. Then add the flour, 1 cup at a time, until the dough forms a ball.

• Turn out the dough onto a floured surface, and gently knead until smooth.

• Grease a large bowl with olive oil. Place the dough in the bowl and roll around to coat. Cover the bowl and set in a warm place. Let rise for 1 hour or until the dough doubles in size.

• Preheat the oven to 425°F.

• Punch down the dough and move it to a floured surface, kneading until smooth. Roll and stretch the dough into a 12-inch diameter. Transfer it to a pizza pan or stone.

• Rub the dough with more olive oil. Use fork tines to poke the dough evenly.

• Spread the pizza sauce evenly over the dough. Top with half the cheese and all of the sausage and mushrooms. Sprinkle on the basil and oregano, and top with the remaining cheese.

• Bake for 17 to 20 minutes.

• Slice to serve. This savory pie is the perfect meal to share with friends who pop by for a visit.

DRAGON'S DINNER BEEF STEW

Inspired by Episode 144: "Lucy Goes to Scotland" (Season 5)

◇◇

IN HER STORYBOOK reverie, Lucy is afraid of becoming the dinner of a two-headed dragon that wakes from its hibernation every thirty years to satiate its appetite with members of the McGillicuddy tribe. To calm her nerves, Ricky serenades her via a romantic love song, in which he sings about being in love with a dragon's dinner. Imagine if the beast was served Scottish beef stew instead! This recipe is made with rich, flavorful stout and is hearty enough to satisfy even a long-hibernating dragon.

MAKES 4 TO 6 SERVINGS

2 pounds beef chuck, cubed

¼ cup all-purpose flour

1½ teaspoons salt, divided

1 teaspoon freshly ground black pepper, divided

2 tablespoons olive oil

2 tablespoons unsalted butter

1 onion, diced

2 carrots, diced

2 celery ribs, diced

1 garlic clove, minced

2 russet potatoes, peeled and diced

2 cups beef stock

1 pint Guinness stout

1 tablespoon thyme

1 tablespoon Worcestershire sauce

1 bay leaf

• Dredge the beef in flour, 1 teaspoon salt, and ½ teaspoon pepper. In a Dutch oven, heat the oil and brown the beef on all sides. Remove and set aside.

• Add the butter to the Dutch oven and sauté the onions, carrots, celery, and garlic, until softened. Return the beef to the pot, along with the potatoes.

• Stir in the beef stock, stout, thyme, Worcestershire sauce, bay leaf, and remaining ½ teaspoons each salt and pepper. Bring to a boil, then lower the heat to low. Cover and simmer for 1½ hours.

• One taste of this savory stew and you'll fall in love with this Dragon's Dinner, too. Try serving this with a Happy Little Loaf of Bread (page 38).

"I'm in love with the dragon's dinner
The dragon's embraceable dinner
I'll swear my love will e'er be true
I'll serve ye with all me heart
But the hungry dragon will serve ye, too
He'll serve ye a la carte"

**—RICKY, IN THE SONG "I'M IN LOVE WITH
THE DRAGON'S DINNER"**

McGILLICUDDY SOUP

Inspired by Episode 144: "Lucy Goes to Scotland" (Season 5)

◇◇

AN ADVENTURE IN Scotland leads to Lucy's dozing off into a fairy-tale dream. In this musical sequence (inspired by the musical Brigadoon!), a dragon awakens every thirty years to frighten a bonny Scottish village unless it's fed a McGillicuddy ancestor. As the last of her kinfolk, Lucy dreads being fed to the dragon as McGillicuddy Soup. This inspired recipe is a version of cock-a-leekie soup, a Scottish dish made with chicken and leeks. The traditional addition of prunes lends a unique sweetness, whose flavor could satiate both mouths of a two-headed dragon.

MAKES 4 SERVINGS

2 pounds bone-in chicken thighs	1 tablespoon parsley
1 onion, chopped	1 bay leaf
2 cans (10.5 ounces) chicken stock	2 teaspoons salt
2 tablespoons lemon juice	1 teaspoon freshly ground black pepper
4 leeks, washed and cut into 1-inch pieces	½ cup prunes, chopped
1 tablespoon thyme	

• In a large pot, bring 1½ quarts water, the chicken, and onion to a boil. Reduce heat to low, cover, and simmer for 1 hour.

• Remove the chicken and discard the bones and skin. Chop the meat and return it to the pot.

• Pour in the chicken stock and lemon juice, and add the leeks, thyme, parsley, bay leaf, salt, and pepper.

• Add the prunes and simmer for another 30 minutes. For peace of mind, know that no McGillicuddys were harmed in the making of this recipe.

TRADITIONAL
ENGLISH SCONES

Inspired by Episode 142: "Lucy Meets the Queen" (Season 5)

LUCY'S ONLY GOAL while in England is to see the Queen. Thinking she'll have a chance as Ricky's guest when his band performs at the Palladium, she spends hours practicing her curtsey to the point of cramping her legs. Undeterred, she decides that her last opportunity to meet Her Majesty would be as a dancer in Ricky's show. Through all the aches and pains, Lucy puts on an unintentionally "comedic" performance that makes quite an impression on the Queen, who asks to meet the lady who did all the humorous dancing. Lucy should have taken time for a spot of tea to relax and work out her charley horse. These English scones are inspired by a proper presentation with Her Majesty. Fluffy and dainty, these morsels won't put a cramp in your afternoon tea.

3 cups all-purpose flour
¼ cup granulated sugar
2 teaspoons baking powder
¼ teaspoon salt
¼ cup (½ stick) cold unsalted butter, cut into cubes

¾ cup whole milk
1 large egg
1 large egg mixed with 1 tablespoon water, for egg wash

• Preheat the oven to 425°F. Prep a baking sheet with a Silpat or parchment paper.

• In a large bowl, whisk the flour, sugar, baking powder, and salt.

• Cut in the butter until it forms fine crumbs. Mix in the milk and egg, just until the dough comes together.

• Turn out the dough onto a floured surface. Roll out to 1 inch thick, and use a 3-inch cutter to cut out circles. Place them on the prepped baking sheet and brush with egg wash.

• Bake for 12 to 14 minutes.

• Let cool. Served with jam and clotted cream, these scones are fit for a queen!

PART FOUR

ENTERTAINING
the
TROPICANA
WAY

THE TROPICANA WAS a second home to Ricky, and scenes involving the club give viewers a glimpse into 1950s nightlife. Later in the series, Ricky purchased the establishment and renamed it Club Babalu, making it all his own.

Dinner, drinks, and dancing were just part of the entertainment offered here. Along with his orchestra, Ricky provided hours of music for the patrons. Those tunes inspired the drinks in this chapter. The rum and cola recipe on page 87 is based on the episode "The Diet," when Lucy is determined to lose weight to fit into a certain outfit that would let her perform "Cuban Pete" with Ricky. The pisco sour is a toast to Lucy and Ricky's hilarious performance of the number "In Santiago, Chile," all while handcuffed to each other in the "Handcuffs" episode. The recipe for a robust take on an Old Cuban cocktail on page 79 was inspired by Little Ricky and his father's dazzling performance of Ricky's signature song in "The Ricardos Visit Cuba." And, of course, creating a recipe around Ricky's most popular ballad, "Babalu," is a must.

Try these recipes along with a few appetizers to re-create the nightlife of the Tropicana in your own home.

"Babalu ayé!"

—RICKY, IN THE
SONG "BABALU"

BABALU

Inspired by Episode 162: "The Ricardos Visit Cuba" (Season 6)

◇◇

WRITTEN IN 1939 by Cuban singer and composer Margarita Lecuona, "Babalu" is a rousing call to the Santería god from which the song takes its name. From the booming baritone of his lyrics to the hypnotic speed of his conga drum, "Babalu" is also Ricky Ricardo's signature song.

No episode features the number better than "The Ricardos Visit Cuba." While Lucy does everything wrong trying to win over Ricky's uncle Alberto, it's Little Ricky and his father's joint rendition of "Babalu" that eventually charms the family patriarch's heart. This drink is inspired by Ricky's popular ballad, a variation on an Old Cuban cocktail—a sweet mix of lime and bitters garnished with mint. This thirst quencher will make you call out, *"Babalu ayé!"*

MAKES 1 DRINK

1 jigger (1½ ounces) Cuban rum	8 fresh mint leaves, plus more for garnish
1 ounce simple syrup	1 cup ice
2 tablespoons freshly squeezed lime juice	2 ounces sparkling wine
2 dashes aromatic bitters	

• In a cocktail shaker, muddle the rum, simple syrup, lime juice, and bitters with the mint leaves.
• Add the ice and shake well.
• Strain into a glass and top with sparkling wine.
• Garnish with a mint leaf and grab your conga drum for a song!

CONGA BITES

Inspired by Episode 6: "The Audition" (Season 1)

◇◇

IF ONLY TIME travel were possible. In the 1950s, nightclubs were the place to be—full of unique entertainment that dazzled, including clowns! In this episode when Buffo the clown gets injured during rehearsal, only Lucy would think to jump into the clown's shoes and take his place. Inspired by this performance, these coconut cream cheese appetizers—a staple of 1950s hors d'oeuvre—will help you imagine a night out at the club, dining on cocktail snacks while enjoying a delightful round of entertainment.

MAKES 15 SERVINGS

2 cups unsweetened coconut flakes	2 slices bacon, cooked and crumbled
8 ounces cream cheese, at room temperature	½ cup minced green bell pepper
	¼ teaspoon onion powder

• Preheat the oven to 350°F. Prep a baking sheet with a Silpat or parchment paper.
• Spread the coconut evenly on the baking sheet. Bake for 5 to 8 minutes, until browned. Let cool.
• In a small bowl, stir together the cream cheese, bacon, bell pepper, and onion powder.
• Form the mixture into 1½-inch round balls.
• Roll the balls in toasted coconut to serve, and party like it's 1955.

HIGH-OCTANE LEMONADE

Featured in Episode 161: "Desert Island" (Season 6)

◇◇

MUCH TO THE girls' chagrin, Ricky and Fred are set to judge a bathing beauty contest later in the afternoon, but first they're all going out to enjoy a day at sea. Lucy comes up with a plan to make sure the boat has only half a tank of gas— just the right amount to strand them long enough for the boys to miss the contest. Her plan is to then save the day by revealing an extra store of gas, some that she's hidden in a jug on the boat. Unbeknownst to her, the plan has been foiled because earlier, Fred found the hidden jug full of gas and, after deeming it a safety hazard, left it behind on the pier. This means Lucy's stranding them at sea is no prank but a real ordeal. Inspired by this signature bit of Lucy-and-Ethel-style mischief, this high-octane lemonade will have you yearning for cold drinks and a day of boating; just make sure you have a way home.

MAKES 10 SERVINGS

¾ cup sugar	2 cups cold water
1 cup lemon juice	1 cup ice, plus more for serving
¾ cup vodka	Sliced lemon, to garnish

• In a saucepan over medium-high heat, cook the sugar and 1 cup water until the sugar is dissolved. Let cool completely.

• In a large pitcher, stir together the simple syrup, lemon juice, vodka, cold water, and ice.

• Pour over glasses filled with ice. To serve, garnish with lemon slices, and enjoy in the sun.

LUCY:

"Ethel, how many times have I ever let you down?"

ETHEL:

"Well, uh ..."

LUCY:

"Never mind!"

IN SANTIAGO, CHILE

Inspired by Episode 37: "The Handcuffs" (Season 2)

◇◇◇

LUCY USES FRED'S old handcuffs to bind herself to Ricky as a prank to spend more time together, of course landing the couple in mayhem when they can't find the key. This situation results in Ricky doing a big television production all while handcuffed, leaving Lucy to give a memorable performance of "In Santiago, Chile"—just as Ricky's spirited right hand. Their sidesplitting routine is the inspiration for this citrusy pisco sour.

MAKES 1 DRINK

1 jigger (1½ ounces) pisco	1 egg white
1 ounce simple syrup	1 cup ice
2 tablespoons freshly squeezed lime juice	2 dashes aromatic bitters, for garnish

• Into a cocktail shaker, pour the pisco, simple syrup, lime juice, and egg white. Shake for 10 seconds. Add the ice, and shake for another 10 to 20 seconds.

• Strain into a chilled glass and garnish with bitters. Serve this drink to someone you'd love to be locked up with.

Note: This recipe contains raw egg. Because of the slight risk of salmonella, raw eggs should not be served to the very young, the ill or elderly, or to pregnant women.

CUBAN PETE

Inspired by Episode 4: "The Diet" (Season 1)

◇◇

RICKY'S MOST FAMOUS song may be "Babalu," but his rendition of "Cuban Pete" will get you on your feet. In this episode, to perform in Ricky's show, Lucy goes on a diet to fit into a perfect size 12 costume. After jumping rope and running laps, she resorts to an old-fashioned sweatbox. The hours in the sauna pay off as Lucy makes it to the show just in time to perform "Sally Sweet" to Ricky's "Cuban Pete." This drink is an ode to the melody—a classic rum and cola.

MAKES 1 DRINK

2 ounces Cuban rum	**Lime wedges, to garnish**
5 ounces cola	

• Fill a highball glass with ice; pour in the rum. Top off with cola. Garnish with lime, to serve. Cool and smooth, just like Ricky Ricardo himself.

SHRIMP COCKTAIL

Featured in Episode 49: "Lucy Changes Her Mind" (Season 2)

◇◇◇

A STAPLE OF 1950s fine dining, shrimp cocktail is the must-have starter before your dinner of choice. In "Lucy Changes Her Mind," the foursome goes out to eat and Lucy, in her indecision, changes her mind about her meal every time someone else orders. When the exasperated waiter offers the option of shrimp cocktail as a starter, Ricky puts a breadstick in Lucy's mouth before she has a chance to consider something different. There'll be no indecision when you make your own version of this appetizer. Fresh prawns served with a spicy horseradish cocktail sauce is unquestionably the most elegant way to start off a meal.

MAKES 4 TO 6 SERVINGS

FOR THE COCKTAIL SAUCE
1 cup chili sauce
3 tablespoons lemon juice
1 tablespoon lemon zest
1 tablespoon prepared horseradish
½ teaspoon hot sauce
¼ teaspoon freshly ground
black pepper
Lemon wedges, for serving

FOR THE SHRIMP
Half of 1 lemon
4 garlic cloves, smashed
1 tablespoon salt
1 bay leaf
1 pound shell-on jumbo shrimp,
deveined

• In a small bowl, whisk together the chili sauce, lemon juice, lemon zest, horseradish, hot sauce, and pepper. Place in the refrigerator until ready to use.
• In a large pot over high heat, bring 2½ quarts water and the lemon, garlic, salt, and bay leaf to a boil.
• Cook the shrimp until they turn pink, about 2 to 3 minutes.
• Remove the shrimp and transfer to a large bowl of ice water to cool. Drain and serve the shrimp on ice with cocktail sauce and lemon. This hors d'oeuvre is so good, it will be your first and only choice every time.

LUAU NIBBLES

Inspired by Episode 161: "Desert Island" (Season 6)

ONLY LUCY COULD start out on a wayward boat ride that ends up on a deserted island with her family, her best friends . . . and Claude Akins. Even though he's dressed as a frightful island native, it's all for show as the island turns out to be the actor's film location. Seeing as how they've wasted a good day off, he invites everyone to a luau wrap party on the beach. Inspired by a festive fete on the sand, these pineapple bacon hors d'oeuvre are a timeless 1950s treat.

MAKES 12 SERVINGS

8 slices thin bacon	2 tablespoons brown sugar
1 (20-ounce) can pineapple chunks, drained	24 pimiento stuffed olives

• Cut the bacon into thirds. Wrap each piece around a pineapple chunk and place on a small skewer.

• Sprinkle with brown sugar and place the skewers on a foil-lined baking sheet. Broil for 5 to 6 minutes, until the bacon becomes dark and crispy.

• Add an olive on the end of each skewer. Serve at your next island-themed party.

Vitameatavegamin

Alcohol 23%

The Taste Treat to Good Health
containing concentrated

vitamins, meat
vegetables and minerals

Adults should take 1 tablespoonful
3 times a day after meals.

Excessively sweet apple pectin was used as a stand-in for Vitameatavegamin and take after take made Lucy queasy!

Vitameatavegamin

"Hello friends! Are you tired, run down, listless? Do you poop out at parties?" Most fans can recite at least some of Lucy's classic TV pitch verbatim. In the episode "Lucy Does a TV Commercial," while trying to prove her acting prowess, Lucy unknowingly becomes intoxicated from a very medicinal "health aid" she's been hired to sell: Vitameatavegamin. That's Vita-meata-vegamin. The serum seems to be a cure for all of life's problems, thanks to ingredients like vitamins, meat, vegetables, and minerals. Missing from the content list is that it also contains 23 percent alcohol.

As Lucy "spoons her way to health" during rehearsals, you can see her start to change from a happy, peppy person to a highly inebriated one! This classic *I Love Lucy* scene showcased the brilliance of Lucille Ball's comedic timing.

Only Lucy could go from a lucid salesperson to tipsy twit and still make you want to have a taste of the magic elixir. The viscous consistency only made the pitch more intriguing. Did it taste like maple syrup or tomato soup? You may never know (unless you're a fan of drinking apple pectin), but Vitameatavegamin's promises live on forever in reruns. In the meantime, you can enjoy a unique take by following the Vitameatavegamin recipe on page 96.

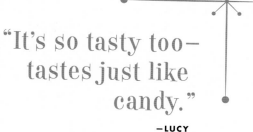

"It's so tasty too—
tastes just like
candy."

—LUCY

*Normally composed,
Lucille Ball was so
nervous about messing
up—particularly the
word Vitameatavegamin—
that she just couldn't
appreciate the humor
in the episode and was
stressed about it before
and during filming.*

VITAMEATAVEGAMIN

Featured in Episode 30: "Lucy Does a TV Commercial" (Season 1)

LUCY'S SALES PITCH for Vitameatavegamin is legendary. Who knew that you could spoon your way to health with a cure-all containing 23 percent alcohol? This version isn't nearly as potent, but will still give you quite a kick! This is a robust Bloody Mary with a garnish of—you guessed it—vitamins, meat, vegetables, and minerals. So if you're tired, run down, listless, if you poop out at parties and are unpopular, then why don't you join the thousands of happy, peppy people and make a glass of your very own Vitameatavegamin today? That's Vita-meata-vegamin.

MAKES 1 DRINK

FOR THE GARNISHES

1 strip bacon

¼ teaspoon brown sugar

⅛ teaspoon freshly ground black pepper

2 to 3 cherry tomatoes

1 lime wedge

1 celery rib

1 carrot

FOR THE DRINK

1 lime wedge

2 tablespoons celery salt

2 cups ice cubes, divided

1½ ounces vodka

1 cup tomato juice

1 teaspoon prepared horseradish

1 teaspoon Worcestershire sauce

1 to 2 dashes hot sauce

1½ tablespoons lemon juice

1 tablespoon freshly squeezed lime juice

⅛ teaspoon freshly ground black pepper

• Run a wooden skewer through the strip of bacon. Sprinkle with brown sugar and pepper, then fry in a pan over medium heat, until crisp. Place the cherry tomatoes on the other end of the skewer, and set aside.

• Rub the rim of a glass with the lime, then dip the rim into a dish of the celery salt.

• Fill the glass with ice. Put the rest of the ice in a cocktail shaker, along with the vodka, tomato juice, horseradish, Worcestershire sauce, hot sauce, lemon juice, lime juice, and pepper. Shake well, then strain into the glass.

• Garnish with the cooked bacon, skewered cherry tomatoes, and lime wedge, celery, and carrot. While there's no guarantee this will help spoon your way to health, it will definitely give your spirits a delightful lift!

PART FIVE

BREAKFAST WITH THE RICARDOS

MORNINGS WITH THE Ricardos included a generous breakfast that often consisted of eggs and bacon along with potatoes or waffles, and sometimes grapefruit. Every once in a while, there would be a wayward appearance of a flying piece of toast popping out of their toaster. Always served on their distinctive Franciscan Ivy dishware, a spread like that was accompanied by freshly squeezed orange juice and cups of coffee.

The recipes in this chapter are all an ode to the Ricardos' love of breakfast. The dish Adam and Eve on a Raft, Wreck 'Em came from Fred's playful diner-speak order of scrambled eggs on toast in "The Diner" episode. Lucy's memorable dance while wearing a shirt stuffed with eggs in "Lucy Does the Tango" inspired the recipe for a Dozen Egg Frittata on page 103. And who can forget Lucy's historic wall climb to grab one of Richard Widmark's grapefruits in "The Tour"? The Richard Widmark Breakfast Grapefruit on page 117 is ideal for eating while daydreaming about your favorite celebrity!

Any of these morning meals created with America's favorite TV foursome in mind would get your day off to the right start.

ADAM AND EVE ON A RAFT, WRECK 'EM

Featured in Episode 92: "The Diner" (Season 3)

◇◇

FRED AND ETHEL know a thing or two about working in a diner, right down to colorful nicknames for popular items on the menu. When the Ricardos and Mertzes go into the restaurant business, it doesn't take long before the couples are at odds. In dividing the diner down the middle, Fred and Ethel's half is renamed "Big Hunk of America." When an order comes in, Fred yells, "Adam and Eve on a raft, wreck 'em!" While it sounds obscure, it's really just a fun code for everyday scrambled eggs on toast!

MAKES 1 SERVING

1 slice French bread	1 tablespoon whole milk
2 teaspoons unsalted butter, at room temperature	⅛ teaspoon salt
1 teaspoon grated Parmesan cheese	⅛ teaspoon freshly ground black pepper
2 large eggs	2 teaspoons olive oil
	½ teaspoon chopped chives

• Spread the butter on the bread and sprinkle with Parmesan cheese. Toast in the toaster until golden brown. Set aside.

• In a medium bowl, whisk together the eggs, milk, salt, and pepper.

• In a pan over medium-low heat, add the olive oil and the eggs. Cook, stirring gently with a spatula, until the eggs are cooked soft.

• Place on toast and sprinkle with chives to serve. No coded yelling necessary.

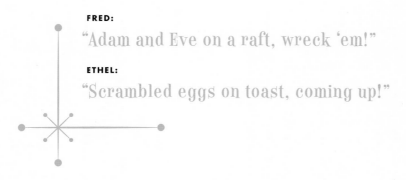

FRED:

"Adam and Eve on a raft, wreck 'em!"

ETHEL:

"Scrambled eggs on toast, coming up!"

DOZEN EGG FRITTATA

Inspired by Episode 172: "Lucy Does the Tango" (Season 6)

◇◇◇

FOOLING RICKY NEVER works out but that doesn't mean Lucy won't stop trying. After going into the egg business, Ricky and Fred begin quarreling, as it seems the hens aren't doing their job. With their friendship on the line, Lucy and Ethel take matters into their own hands and purchase a stash of eggs. To cover up their scheme, Lucy must smuggle the fresh eggs out to the henhouse in her clothes. Caught off guard by Ricky when he suddenly calls a rehearsal of their PTA tango performance right then and there, the dance culminates in a powerful torso-to-torso finale that leaves Lucy with a shirt full of smashed eggs. When life gives you eggs? How about a delicious frittata?

1 dozen large eggs
½ cup heavy whipping cream
2 teaspoons garlic powder
1½ teaspoons onion powder
1½ teaspoons salt
1 teaspoon freshly ground black pepper

1 tablespoon olive oil
1 cup sliced mushrooms
1 garlic clove, minced
1 cup cooked and crumbled bacon
½ cup cooked spinach
1 cup shredded Cheddar cheese

• In a medium bowl, whisk together the eggs, heavy whipping cream, garlic powder, onion powder, salt, and pepper. Set aside.

• In a large ovenproof skillet over medium-high heat, add the olive oil and sauté the mushrooms and garlic, until soft.

• Add the bacon and spinach, then pour the egg mixture into the skillet.

• Sprinkle with cheese and cook until the edges are just set.

• Broil in the oven for 2 to 3 minutes, until the egg is set in the middle. When preparing this recipe it is advisable to transport your eggs in cartons rather than your clothing.

LUCY:

"Honey, if we're gonna dance for the PTA we should be dignified. We should stand at least two feet apart."

RICKY:

"To tango?!"

EGGS BENEDICT

Featured in Episode 24: "The Gossip" (Season 1)

SOMETIMES A PIECE of gossip is so juicy you just can't help yourself. Ricky is tired of Lucy spreading rumors, and believes women are just natural gossipers. Out to prove him wrong, Lucy and Ethel bet Ricky and Fred that the women can stop gossiping longer than the men, with the winners to be served breakfast in bed for a month. Hoping to prompt a quick failure from the ladies, Ricky and Fred make up a phony story about neighbor Grace Foster running away with the milkman. When Lucy and Ethel fall victim to the prank, the boys think they've won, but are stunned when Mr. Foster storms in chasing after the milkman. It turns out Lucy was one step ahead, paying off the two men for their performances. Thus ensuring their win, the gals order up a stunning breakfast of honeydew melon filled with strawberries; eggs Benedict; and hot chocolate. Now you can make your own version of this winning meal—just remember to keep the rumors to yourself.

FOR THE POACHED EGGS
4 large eggs
2 tablespoons white vinegar

FOR THE HOLLANDAISE SAUCE
4 egg yolks
1 cup (2 sticks) unsalted butter, cubed
2 tablespoons lemon juice

¼ teaspoon salt

FOR THE ASSEMBLY
2 English muffins, split
2 tablespoons unsalted butter, at room temperature
4 slices Canadian bacon
1 tablespoon chopped parsley

- Crack each egg into its own ramekin.
- In a large pot over medium-high heat, bring 1½ quarts water to a low simmer. Stir in the vinegar.
- Slip one egg into the water. Cook until the white firms up, about 1 minute.
- Remove the egg with a slotted spoon, and let drain on a plate lined with paper towels. Repeat with the rest of the eggs.
- Prep a double boiler with water, and bring to a simmer over medium heat.
- In the top half of the double boiler, whisk the egg yolks. Add the cubed butter while whisking constantly. Once all the butter has been incorporated, stir in the lemon juice and salt.
- Toast the English muffins and spread butter on top.
- In a pan over medium-high heat, add the Canadian bacon slices and cook until slightly browned.
- Place the Canadian bacon on the buttered English muffins. Top with a poached egg, and a spoonful of Hollandaise sauce.
- Sprinkle with parsley, to garnish. Enjoy on a tray from the comfort of your bed, preferably alongside a partner to gab with—minus the gossip.

LUCY:

"Me, gossip?"

RICKY:

"What do you call what you were doing on the phone?"

LUCY:

"Well it wasn't gossiping. I prefer to think of it as a mutual exchange of vital information."

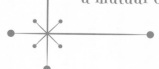

ICED COFFEE

Featured in Episode 33: "Lucy's Schedule" (Season 1)

◇◇◇

KEEPING TO A strict schedule imposed on her by Ricky means that Lucy has to cut some corners—a point Lucy goes to great lengths to make by preparing Ricky's morning cup o' joe ahead of time and freezing it for future use. Lucy was truly a trailblazer, as iced coffee is, of course, an extremely popular refreshment today. This take on a café Cubano uses coffee ice cubes, ensuring that the energy-boosting brew stays strong and delicious.

MAKES 1 CUP

1 cup coffee, at room temperature	1 shot espresso, cooled
2 teaspoons granulated sugar	⅓ cup whole milk

- Pour the coffee into an ice cube tray. Freeze overnight until solid.
- Place the sugar in a glass, followed by the ice cubes.
- Add the espresso, top off with milk. With this morning boost, you'll be checking items off your to-do list in no time.

LUCY'S FAVORITE WAFFLES

Featured in Episode 51: "Pregnant Women Are Unpredictable" (Season 2)

◇◇

WANTING TO DOTE on your pregnant wife is admirable, but not when it makes more work for her in the long run. Determined to cook Lucy's favorite breakfast, Ricky runs into trouble in the kitchen, resulting in total chaos. Even if you make a mess, don't worry about it; these fluffy waffles will make up for it.

2 cups all-purpose flour
2 tablespoons brown sugar
2½ teaspoons baking powder
½ teaspoon cinnamon
¼ teaspoon salt

1½ cups buttermilk
2 large eggs
1½ tablespoons unsalted butter, melted

- Prep your waffle maker according to the manufacturer's directions.
- In a small bowl, whisk together the flour, brown sugar, baking powder, cinnamon, and salt.
- Make a well in the center of the dry ingredients and add the buttermilk, eggs, and melted butter. Stir until just combined.
- Pour the batter into the waffle maker and cook until browned. Serve with syrup and fresh fruit, and your pregnant partner will appreciate your efforts.

RICKY:

"Now Lucy, I don't care what you name the baby but we've got to get it settled."

LUCY:

"Well I'm not gonna settle on just any old thing, I want the names to be unique and euphonious."

RICKY:

"Okay, Unique if it's a boy and Euphonius if it's a girl."

When Lucy gets trapped in Richard Widmark's house, she tries to disguise herself as a mounted trophy.

RICHARD WIDMARK
BREAKFAST GRAPEFRUIT

Inspired by Episode 127: "The Tour" (Season 4)

◇◇

LUCY'S MOMENTS IN Los Angeles are some of the most memorable, especially her run-ins with the stars. After running into William Holden, Eve Arden, and Rock Hudson, she simply must complete her celebrity souvenir collection by grabbing a prized grapefruit from Richard Widmark's backyard. That star grapefruit is the inspiration for this simple breakfast, which gets a lift from a touch of warm cinnamon, sugar, and a pinch of salt that Lucy always adds to her morning citrus, to cut the sourness. Autographed grapefruits don't last forever, so you might as well fix this one up for breakfast.

Half a grapefruit, segmented
2 teaspoons brown sugar
¼ teaspoon cinnamon

⅛ teaspoon salt
Mint leaf, for garnish

- Sprinkle the grapefruit half with brown sugar and cinnamon.
- Place in a heatproof dish and broil 3 to 4 minutes, just until the sugar starts to bubble.
- Sprinkle with salt. Garnish with a mint leaf to serve. This would be the perfect accompaniment to a Robert Taylor orange!

"Gee, I'd love to have a Richard Widmark grapefruit to go with my Robert Taylor orange."

—LUCY

FRIED EGG SANDWICH

Featured in Episode 54: "Ricky Has Labor Pains" (Season 2)

◇◇

WHEN THERE'S ABOUT to be a new addition to the family, sometimes the husband develops pregnancy symptoms even more than the expectant wife. While enceinte, Lucy is a little consumed with impending motherhood, so she understandingly skips a few daily chores, leaving Ricky to feel like a forgotten man. When she neglects to cook the roast beef she intended to make him for dinner, she offers up a fried egg sandwich as a substitute. This is an excellent easy dinner for new parents in need of a quick bite, or for a husband who's feeling his own labor pains.

MAKES 1 SANDWICH

2 slices country French bread	⅛ teaspoon salt
2 tablespoons unsalted butter, divided	⅛ teaspoon freshly ground black pepper
2 large eggs	2 slices white Cheddar cheese

- Lightly toast the bread, then spread with 1 tablespoon butter. Set aside.
- In a skillet over medium-high heat, add the remaining butter. When the butter is melted, crack the eggs into the pan and season with salt and pepper.
- When the whites begin to set, flip the eggs over. Cook until the whites are completely set.
- Place the eggs on top of one piece of toast. Top with cheese, then the second piece of toast.
- Slice to serve to a harried husband, or, better yet, an expectant mom.

RICKY'S TAKEOUT BREAKFAST

Featured in Episode 39: "Job Switching" (Season 2)

IN "JOB SWITCHING," Lucy and Ricky swap roles—she goes to work while Ricky endeavors to stay home and take care of the house. He quickly learns that waking up and cooking a perfect breakfast for your spouse isn't easy. In fact, sometimes it's impossible. Desperate to cover up his kitchen failures, Ricky picks up two breakfasts to go from the corner drugstore, which include eggs, potatoes, toast, and coffee. Still, a hot breakfast is a hot breakfast, no matter who makes it.

FOR THE POTATOES

2 tablespoons unsalted butter

½ onion, diced

½ cup diced green bell pepper

1 clove garlic, minced

1 tablespoon olive oil

4 russet potatoes, peeled and cubed

1 teaspoon salt

½ teaspoon onion powder

¼ teaspoon freshly ground black pepper

FOR THE EGGS

1 tablespoon unsalted butter

2 large eggs

⅛ teaspoon salt

⅛ teaspoon freshly ground black pepper

• In a skillet over medium-high heat, melt the butter, and sauté the onion, bell pepper, and garlic, until softened.

• Add the olive oil and potatoes. Cook until browned on all sides.

• Season with salt, onion powder, and pepper. Set aside.

• In a pan over medium heat, melt the butter and crack the eggs into the pan. Season with salt and pepper.

• Once the whites start to set, flip over and cook for 4 to 5 more seconds.

• Plate the eggs with the potatoes and serve along with toast and coffee. Enjoy this hearty meal before heading off to a long day at work.

PART SIX

DELECTABLE DESSERTS

ANY GOOD MEAL feels more complete when there's a scrumptious dessert waiting for you at the end. Pastries, pudding, pie, you name it—sweets make the world a better place. *I Love Lucy* features its fair share of confections, and this chapter showcases some of the best.

In "First Stop," as the Ricardos and Mertzes travel west to Hollywood, they encounter a series of signs advertising Aunt Sally's Pecan Pralines, making them all long for a bite of the sweet morsels. Alas, they never get to taste those treats, but now you can with the recipe on page 133! The Aloha Cream Pie on page 124 takes inspiration from "Ricky's Hawaiian Vacation," and a Friends of the Friendless Dessert for One on page 129 will keep you from feeling lonely on your birthday or any day of the year.

If you have a sweet tooth and love Lucy, this is the chapter for you.

ALOHA CREAM PIE

Inspired by Episode 88: "Ricky's Hawaiian Vacation" (Season 3)

WHEN RICKY AND his band are scheduled for a quick gig in Hawaii, Lucy is desperate to go. She hatches a plan and writes to *The Freddie Filmore Show* about the Mertzes, a penniless couple who take care of their feeble old Mother Mertz (actually Lucy in disguise!). They are invited to appear on the show, along with Lucy, to try and win a trip to Hawaii. Of course, winning a free trip is never that easy. In order to win the trip Lucy must stand in place while Ricky sings songs, with the key words being items that fall from the sky in her direction, one of them being a load of cream pie. This Hawaiian-themed dessert is an ode to Lucy's willingness to do anything for a trip to the islands.

MAKES 8 SERVINGS

FOR THE PIE
1 round prepared pie dough
⅓ cup sweetened flaked coconut
¼ cup macadamia nuts, minced
¼ cup crushed pineapple,
well drained

FOR THE FILLING
1 can (14 ounces) coconut milk
1½ cups heavy whipping cream
3 large egg yolks
¾ cup granulated sugar

½ cup cornstarch
½ cup sweetened flaked coconut
1 teaspoon coconut extract
½ teaspoon vanilla
¼ teaspoon salt

FOR THE WHIPPED CREAM
1½ cups heavy whipping cream
¼ cup confectioners' sugar
1 teaspoon vanilla
½ teaspoon coconut extract
¼ teaspoon salt

- Preheat the oven to 425°F.
- Roll out the pie dough into a 9-inch pie dish. Prick the bottom and sides of the crust with a fork. Bake for 7 to 8 minutes. Let cool.
- Lower the heat in the oven to 350°F. Line a baking sheet with parchment paper.
- Spread the coconut on the baking sheet and bake until browned, about 6 to 8 minutes. Let cool.
- In a double boiler over medium-high heat, simmer the coconut milk and heavy whipping cream until bubbles form along the edges. Reduce the heat and add the egg yolks, sugar, and cornstarch, whisking constantly until thickened, approximately 7 to 8 minutes.
- Remove from the heat, and stir in the coconut, coconut extract, vanilla, and salt.
- Pour the filling into the pie shell. Refrigerate 6 hours or overnight.
- In the bowl of an electric mixer fitted with the whisk attachment, whip the heavy whipping cream, confectioners' sugar, vanilla, coconut extract, and salt, until stiff peaks start to form.
- Top the pie with the whipped cream, toasted coconut, macadamia nuts, and pineapple, to serve. While it may not be a trip to Hawaii, this pie will give you the sense of being in the islands, without having to play any games.

LUCY:

"Now, Ethel, the minute I won that trip, I was going to ask them to let me take Fred and Ethel Mertz with me."

ETHEL:

"Oh, sure!"

LUCY:

"I was, and if I couldn't take you with me, I was going to send you a postcard."

FRIENDS OF THE FRIEND-LESS DESSERT FOR ONE

Inspired by Episode 60: "Lucy's Last Birthday" (Season 2)

◇◇

BIRTHDAYS CAN BE a lot of fun—that is, unless all your loved ones seem to have forgotten the big day. When Lucy comes to just that conclusion, she goes for a walk and happens upon the Friends of the Friendless, a group that takes in those who have no one. In the end, Lucy goes down to the club to let Ricky have it, but she walks into a surprise party for her that was being planned all along. Still, if you ever feel like "flotsam in the sea of life, a pitiful outcast shunned by your fellow man," this retro baked Alaska dessert for one will lift your spirits.

MAKES 1 SERVING

1 slice pound cake, 1 inch thick	¼ teaspoon vanilla
1 scoop raspberry sorbet	3 tablespoons confectioners' sugar
2 egg whites	⅛ teaspoon salt
¼ teaspoon cream of tartar	

• Use a 3-inch cutter to cut out a circle from the pound cake. Add a scoop of raspberry sorbet on top. Place in the freezer until ready to serve.

• In a large bowl, use a hand mixer to beat the egg whites, cream of tartar, and vanilla.

• Sprinkle in the confectioners' sugar and salt. Continue beating until stiff peaks form.

• Remove the ice cream from the freezer. Place meringue mixture in a piping bag and pipe around the ice cream, making sure to cover the cake on the bottom.

• Preheat the oven to 500°F. Bake until the meringue peaks are golden brown, about 2 minutes. If you make this sweet treat, you will never again be friendless because you'll have this dessert by your side.

"If you accept our friendship, you will never again be friendless, for we are the Friends of the Friendless and you will have friends."

CHOCOLATE BROWNIES

Featured in Episode 80: "Ricky Minds the Baby" (Season 3)

WHEN FRED AND Ethel come to visit, Lucy offers them some brownies with the warning that they're a little stale. Actually, they're more like bricks. As the Mertzes settle in, they learn that Ricky has a whole week off from work and Lucy wants him to spend more time with Little Ricky. Afraid a fight is about to start, Ethel considers grabbing the brownies to keep them from being used as weapons! But her caution is unnecessary, as Ricky surprisingly agrees and can't wait to care for the baby. The brownies made from this recipe could never be used as weapons, and as a bonus, they're perfect for snacking on while chasing after a little one.

MAKES 12 SERVINGS

1 cup all-purpose flour

1 cup unsweetened cocoa powder

2 cups granulated sugar

½ teaspoon baking powder

½ teaspoon salt

1 cup (2 sticks) unsalted butter, melted, plus more as needed for the pan

3 large eggs

1 teaspoon vanilla

¾ cup chocolate chips

• Preheat the oven to 350°F. Grease and flour a 13- x 9-inch baking pan.

• In a large bowl, whisk together the flour, cocoa powder, sugar, baking powder, and salt.

• Make a well in the center of the mixture and stir in the butter, eggs, and vanilla. Next, stir in the chocolate chips.

• Pour the mixture into the prepped pan and bake for 25 to 30 minutes.

• Let cool, then slice and serve. These brownies are so good they won't even have time to get stale!

AUNT SALLY'S PECAN PRALINES

Featured in Episode 111: "First Stop" (Season 4)

◇◇

DURING THEIR CROSS-COUNTRY road trip to Hollywood, every few miles the Ricardos and Mertzes spot advertisements for Aunt Sally's Pecan Pralines. Sign after sign, they grow more intrigued by the sweet-sounding candy. Unfortunately, the final sign reads "Out of Business"! No matter; you can get a taste for yourself with this recipe for delicious, mouthwatering candy pralines.

MAKES 24 SERVINGS

2 cups brown sugar, packed	1 teaspoon vanilla
⅔ cup heavy whipping cream	¼ teaspoon salt
¼ cup (½ stick) unsalted butter	1½ cups chopped pecans

- Line two baking sheets with Silpats or parchment paper. Set aside.
- In a Dutch oven over medium-high heat, stir together the brown sugar, heavy whipping cream, and butter. Bring to a boil until the mixture reaches the soft ball stage, 235°F on a candy thermometer.
- Remove from heat and stir in the vanilla and salt. Let cool slightly. Stir in the pecans, then drop by the scoopful (approximately 3 tablespoons) onto the lined baking sheet.
- Let cool and enjoy the sweet goodness the Ricardos and Mertzes missed on their journey west.

FRED MERTZ'S SEVEN-LAYER (GIVE OR TAKE) CHOCOLATE CAKE

Featured in Episode 39: "Job Switching" (Season 2)

◇◇

BOASTING THAT THEY can do housework better than the gals, Ricky and Fred get ready to tackle their duties. Pooling their talents, they decide to split dinner duties, with Ricky handling the entrée and Fred taking on dessert. His intention is to make a "big juicy cake—seven layers thick." What he shows up with looks more like a pancake, but it's guaranteed this recipe will lead you to a better end result.

MAKES 16 SERVINGS

FOR THE CAKE

4 cups all-purpose flour

1¼ cups unsweetened cocoa powder

3 teaspoons baking soda

½ teaspoon salt

1¼ cups (2½ sticks) unsalted butter, plus extra for greasing pans

2½ cups granulated sugar

4 large eggs

2½ cups buttermilk

½ cup coffee, at room temperature

1 teaspoon vanilla

FOR THE FROSTING

3 cups heavy whipping cream

3 cups semisweet chocolate chips

1 teaspoon vanilla

¼ teaspoon salt

• Preheat the oven to 350°F. Grease and line up to seven 9-inch-round cake pans with parchment paper, then grease the parchment, or wash and reuse pans after each bake to make seven layers.

• In a large bowl, whisk together the flour, cocoa powder, baking soda, and salt. Set aside.

• In the bowl of an electric mixer, cream the butter and sugar. Add the eggs until combined.

• Alternate adding the dry ingredients with the buttermilk and coffee. Next, stir in the vanilla.

• Bake each cake for 15 minutes, or until a toothpick tester comes out clean. Remove from the oven, let cool 10 to 15 minutes or until cake is cool enough to handle, invert onto a wire rack, and let cool completely. Wash and reuse pan if needed.

- In a large saucepan over medium-high heat, bring the heavy whipping cream to a simmer.
- Place the chocolate chips in a medium bowl and pour the heavy whipping cream over them. Let the chocolate soften, then whisk until smooth. Whisk in the vanilla and salt. Let sit for 20 minutes, or until slightly cooled and thickened.
- Place one cake on a plate. Pour $\frac{1}{2}$ cup of icing to cover the layer, then top with a second cake. Repeat until all seven layers are stacked and frosted. Follow this recipe correctly and you'll get to bite into a lovely sized cake, right after you've finished all your housework.

Lucy and Ethel vs. The Chocolates

While the boys stay home and tend to the house, Lucy and Ethel head out into the workforce to get jobs and end up at Kramer's Kandy Kitchen. At first they are separated, with Lucy being placed in the dipping room with an expert candy maker. While the dunking of chocolate seems easy enough, a rogue insect messes up the whole process, resulting in a hilarious chocolatey mess. Meanwhile, Ethel's curiosity gets the better of her when she keeps pinching the chocolates to see what kind they are, resulting in her being booted from the boxing contingent of the factory.

The circumstances don't improve much when the gals are reunited in the wrapping department. As the chocolates roll down the conveyor belt, each is to be wrapped in paper before heading to the next station. If one piece of chocolate gets past them and arrives in the packing room unwrapped—they're fired. What could be simpler than wrapping up chocolates?

They're already behind on wrapping when their supervisor makes the infamous call to "speed it up a little!" Unable to keep up with the new pace, the girls have no choice but to cover their tracks, scooping chocolates into their hats and uniforms, and even stuffing their mouths. It's every chocolate lover's fantasy gone wrong. What seemed like a dream job has turned into sugar-filled agony of hysterical proportions.

KRAMER'S KANDY KITCHEN CHOCOLATE BONBONS

Featured in Episode 39: "Job Switching" (Season 2)

◇◇◇

ARGUABLY THE MOST famous Lucy caper of all time, Lucy and Ethel get jobs at Kramer's Kandy Kitchen, with disastrous results. Who knew chocolate-making could be so achingly hilarious to watch? After an unfortunate spin in the chocolate room coating candies, things go even more awry in the wrapping department, leading to a deliciously chocolatey test of speed and agility.

These bonbons will have you coating candies like a pro in no time. You should have no problem taking the smooth ganache filling and coating it with melted bittersweet chocolate, then topping it off with a garnish of your choice. Almost too easy to make, these beauties won't give you any trouble when wrapping them up.

MAKES 18 CHOCOLATES

FOR THE FILLING
½ cup heavy whipping cream
8 ounces semisweet chocolate, finely chopped
3 tablespoons unsalted butter, cubed
½ teaspoon vanilla

FOR THE COATING
16 ounces bittersweet chocolate, chopped
¼ cup nuts, sea salt, or dried fruit, for the topping decoration

- In a saucepan over low heat, add the cream and bring to a simmer, then remove from heat. Whisk in the semisweet chocolate. Next, add the butter and vanilla, stirring until smooth.
- Pour the mixture into a medium bowl and let cool completely. Cover and chill in the refrigerator for 3 to 4 hours.
- Line a baking sheet with parchment paper. Use a small scoop to form balls of the refrigerated chocolate. Arrange the balls about 1 inch apart on the lined baking sheet and place in the freezer for 10 minutes.
- In a double boiler, melt half the bittersweet chocolate. Remove from heat and stir in the remaining chocolate.
- Use a fork to dip the balls into the melted chocolate. Let set on the parchment-lined baking sheet. Add a small sprinkle of topping for decoration.
- When the chocolate is set, the bonbons are ready to serve. No need to stuff them in your face all at once, but if you can't resist, just make another batch!

KK
_K_

VANILLA CREAM
FRUIT

NE

MER'S
Kitchen

CHOCOLATE BON BONS
TOPPINGS

FACTORY FOREWOMAN:

"Ricardo, I'm going to put you to work chocolate-dipping.
You say you've had experience?"

LITTLE RICKY ICE CREAM SUNDAE

Inspired by Episode 80: "Ricky Minds the Baby" (Season 3)

◇◇

AS BUSY AS he is, Ricky loves being with the baby, and in this episode he even takes over daily duties from Lucy so that he can spend more time with his son. Unfortunately Little Ricky goes missing on Ricky's watch, when he crawls down the hall to the Mertzes, only to be found by a distressed Lucy. To teach Ricky a lesson, she calls him to check on Little Ricky, knowing full well the baby is nowhere to be found in their apartment. Ricky and Fred panic, but in a case of switcheroo, Fred happens upon Little Ricky and brings him back to the apartment. Lucy and Ricky are both dumbfounded, but all is well.

Like father and son, this dessert is a pint-sized version of a standard ice cream sundae. It's also a nod to Fred's advice that every time a kid wanders away, just go down and look in the police station and you find them there eating an ice-cream cone.

MAKES 1 SERVING

¼ cup vanilla ice cream	2 tablespoons whipped cream
1 tablespoon chocolate sauce	1 maraschino cherry

• Scoop the ice cream into a glass. Top with chocolate sauce, whipped cream, and the cherry. When making this recipe, try to keep an eye on the kids, too.

BETTY RAMSAY'S ANGEL FOOD CAKE

Inspired by Episode 175: "Housewarming" (Season 6)

◇◇◇

AFTER MOVING TO the country, Lucy gets to know her new neighbor, Betty Ramsay. Feeling a tad jealous, Ethel finds Lucy's new chum to be snobby, especially since Betty neglects to invite Ethel to her dinner party. Determined to bring her two friends closer together, Lucy invites both of them over, only to see a fast friendship between Betty and Ethel blossom before her very eyes. Lucy finds herself as the third wheel. All is forgiven when the two throw an unexpected surprise housewarming for Lucy and Ricky. Inspired by Betty's dinner party dessert that used Lucy and Ethel's farm-fresh eggs, this angel food cake is so heavenly, it will surely bring everyone closer together.

MAKES 10 TO 12 SERVINGS

9 egg whites, at room temperature	1½ cups granulated sugar
1 teaspoon cream of tartar	1 cup cake flour
1 teaspoon vanilla extract	½ teaspoon salt
½ teaspoon almond extract	

• In the bowl of an electric mixer fitted with the whisk attachment, beat the egg whites until they form soft peaks.

• Stir in the cream of tartar, vanilla extract, and almond extract. Next, add the sugar, very slowly. Fold in the flour and salt.

• Pour the mixture into an ungreased tube pan. Place in a cold oven, then set to 325°F. Bake for 1 hour.

• Invert the cake and let cool in the pan.

• When cooled completely, run a knife along the edges and remove the cake from the pan to serve. Slice and share this cake with all your new neighbors, or bring your two closest pals together and split it three ways.

COUNTRY CLUB SOUFFLÉ SALAD

Inspired by Episode 177: "Country Club Dance" (Season 6)

◇◇◇

AS THE RICARDOS head out to meet their friends Grace and Harry Munson at the country club, along with the Mertzes and the Ramsays, the husbands complain of being dragged to the club's evening dances. But suddenly they become over-enthusiastic when Grace's captivating cousin (a young pre–*I Dream of Jeannie* Barbara Eden) shows up. The next day the men regret their actions, and try to make amends. The couples head back to the club and the husbands dote dutifully on their wives. They all enjoy a night of feasting and frolicking, until the girls suspect there's something afoot, resulting in misunderstandings galore. Inspired by these antics, this fruity soufflé salad is just like the tantalizing array of treats you'd find at country clubs, and its flavor will keep you dining and dancing all night. If only the couples had just concentrated on the buffet tables!

"Fred hasn't been this nice to me since he thought my aunt left me $500."

—ETHEL

MAKES 10 TO 12 SERVINGS

½ cup boiling water
1 package (3 ounces) orange gelatin
½ cup cold water
4 cups miniature marshmallows
1 can (15 ounces) mandarin oranges, drained

1 can (8 ounces) pineapple tidbits, drained
1 box (3.4 ounces) instant vanilla pudding
1 container (8 ounces) frozen whipped topping, thawed

• In a medium bowl, stir together the boiling water and orange gelatin. Stir until the gelatin is dissolved.

• Stir in the cold water and place in the refrigerator to chill for 20 minutes.

• In a separate large bowl, toss together marshmallows, mandarin oranges, pineapple, and vanilla pudding mix. Fold in the whipped topping and orange gelatin mixture.

• Refrigerate overnight. Serve this dish at a festive party so your guests can enjoy it in between dances.

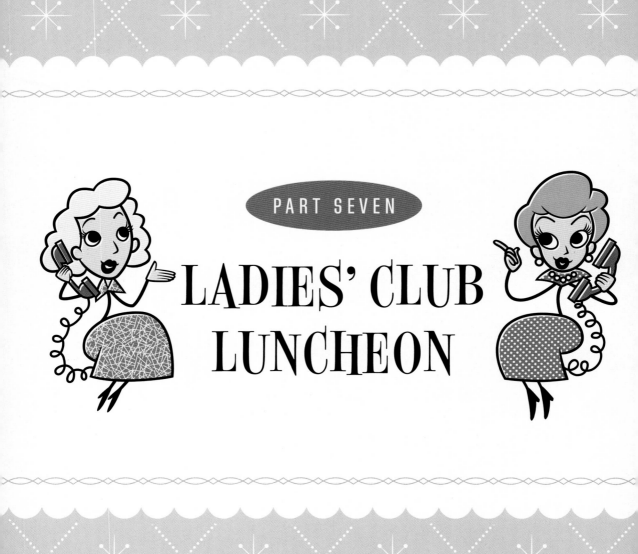

PART SEVEN

LADIES' CLUB LUNCHEON

LADIES' SOCIAL CLUBS were especially popular in the 1950s. In these groups, women met up to plan fundraisers and support causes, but more importantly, it allowed them to get together and mingle with their peers. Lucy and Ethel were members of the Wednesday Afternoon Fine Arts League, which usually met on Tuesday but sometimes they'd meet on Friday. But never mind the name or meeting date, it was the socializing that mattered—and the food. The items in this chapter are all bites that might have been served at these meetups.

In the "Club Election" episode, Lucy and Ethel go toe-to-toe vying for the title of club president. Might the women have nibbled on Deviled Eggs (page 151) while contemplating their vote? When Lucy comes back from her overseas vacation in the episode "Return Home from Europe," she disguises her large cheese as a baby (to avoid paying a baggage fee). If she had been successful in this tricky endeavor, she could have used that in an Italian Cheese Log recipe like the one you'll find on page 154—a savory appetizer perfect for any luncheon.

Using these recipes for scrumptious party snacks, you'll be assured of hosting a successful gathering of all your lady friends.

DEVILED EGGS

Inspired by Episode 47: "The Club Election" (Season 2)

◇◇

THE WEDNESDAY AFTERNOON Fine Arts League is all about decorum and etiquette; that is, until an election is proposed—then it's all-out war. Lucy and Ethel end up as candidates going against each other for the position of president, resulting in a smear campaign like no other as the girls battle it out to gather votes. For such political meetings, refreshments are in order, and this retro deviled egg dish is a staple of lunch gatherings. They're the perfect bite for when you're trying to make an important decision.

MAKES 16 SERVINGS

8 large eggs
3 to 4 tablespoons mayonnaise
1 teaspoon yellow mustard
¼ teaspoon celery salt
¼ teaspoon onion powder

¼ teaspoon salt
⅛ teaspoon freshly ground black pepper
8 pimiento-stuffed olives, cut in half

• Place the eggs in a pot and cover them with 1 to 2 inches of water. Set the heat to medium-high and bring to a boil.
• Turn off the heat, cover with a lid, and let sit for 12 minutes.
• Place the eggs in an ice bath and let cool completely.
• Shell the eggs, then slice in half. Scoop out and set aside the yolks.
• In a medium bowl, stir together the egg yolks, mayonnaise, mustard, celery salt, onion powder, salt, and pepper.
• Place the mixture in a piping bag and pipe the filling into the egg white centers.
• Place an olive half on top of each egg, to garnish. Serve this crowd-pleaser at your next luncheon; it's sure to break up any disagreement that may arise.

ITALIAN CHEESE LOG

Inspired by Episode 153: "Return Home from Europe" (Season 5)

ON THEIR FLIGHT home from Europe, to avoid paying a baggage fee for excess weight, Lucy dresses up her oversized Italian cheese as a baby in order to get it on the plane. A reasonable idea if there ever was one. It turns out her plans were all for naught, as babies don't travel for free either, leading Lucy to find the most creative ways to dispose of the cheese before the plane touches down. This cheese log, inspired by Lucy's adventures in the sky, is also dressed up and ready to be served—no questions asked.

MAKES 6 TO 8 SERVINGS

5 ounces cream cheese, at room temperature	¼ teaspoon onion powder
5 ounces goat cheese, at room temperature	¼ teaspoon salt
1 tablespoon chopped parsley	⅛ teaspoon freshly ground black pepper
1 teaspoon oregano	⅓ cup pistachios, chopped
¼ teaspoon garlic powder	⅓ cup cranberries, chopped

- In a medium bowl, mix together the cream cheese, goat cheese, parsley, oregano, garlic powder, onion powder, salt, and pepper.
- Wrap the mixture in plastic wrap, forming a log. Freeze for 20 minutes.
- Toss the pistachios and cranberries together on a dish. Unwrap the cheese log and roll in the nutty-cran mixture, covering all of the cheese.
- Serve with crackers, not a baby bonnet.

FLUFFY BISCUITS

Featured in Episode 15: "Lucy Plays Cupid" (Season 1)

◇◇

WHETHER YOU'RE TRYING to impress a suitor or entertain friends, these biscuits will attract attention. In "Lucy Plays Cupid," the Ricardos' neighbor Miss Lewis has a crush on the grocer, Mr. Ritter, and Lucy decides to do her best to get the two together. Misunderstanding the situation, Mr. Ritter thinks it's Lucy who has a yen for him. Over a dinner "date," she tries to change Mr. Ritter's heartthrob to heartburn by appearing disheveled, having an unkempt house, and making the worst food imaginable. Selling him on supposedly fluffy biscuits, they arrive hard as rocks. Unlike those decoys, this recipe makes biscuits that are light and airy, and like any good relationship, they're worth the work.

MAKES 10 SERVINGS

2 cups all-purpose flour

1 tablespoon baking powder

1 teaspoon salt

1 teaspoon granulated sugar

6 tablespoons cold unsalted butter, cut into cubes

1 cup buttermilk

1 tablespoon unsalted butter, melted, for brushing

- Preheat the oven to 450°F. Prep a baking sheet with a Silpat or parchment paper.
- In a large bowl, whisk the flour, baking powder, salt, and sugar.
- With a pastry cutter or fork, cut the butter into the flour until it resembles a coarse meal.
- Mix in the buttermilk until just combined. This is a wet dough.
- Turn the dough out onto a floured surface and pat out to 1 inch thick. Fold the dough in half, turn it, and pat it out again. Do this for a total of five times to create layers.
- Use a 3-inch-round cutter to cut out circles. Next, place on the prepped sheets and brush with melted butter.
- Bake for 10 to 12 minutes or until golden brown. Serve these biscuits with creamy butter and fresh jam. They are so good, you're sure to fall in love.

STUFFED CELERY

Inspired by Episode 4: "The Diet" (Season 1)

◇◇

LOSING WEIGHT IS a true battle of the bulge, but Lucy is determined to fit into a costume so she can claim a part in Ricky's show. After a long day of working out, Ethel serves Ricky and Fred steak and potatoes for dinner, while a starving Lucy is handed a single stalk of celery. Throughout the meal the boys hand off scraps to Butch the dog, who's sitting under the table, so naturally Lucy sidles down there to grab a bite too, to no avail. This celery would have offered her a little more sustenance, but it wouldn't be great for dieting, seeing as it's stuffed with delicious, velvety cream cheese.

MAKES 8 SERVINGS

8 celery ribs, washed and
ends cut off

8 ounces cream cheese, at room
temperature

1 tablespoon parsley

½ teaspoon garlic salt

½ teaspoon freshly ground
black pepper

¼ teaspoon onion powder

• Cut the celery into 3-inch pieces. Set aside.
• In a medium bowl, stir together the cream cheese, parsley, garlic salt, pepper, and onion powder.
• Pipe the cheese mixture into the celery sticks to serve, and enjoy heartily. Diet can start tomorrow.

RICKY:

"Honey, so you gained
a little weight. Is that
so terrible?"

LUCY:

"A little weight?
I walked into this room
weighing 110. I now
weigh 132. That's 22
pounds in ten minutes."

ETHEL:
"Fred, you know me, you know how I get on water. I'll be hungry and thirsty and cranky."

FRED:
"What's your excuse on dry land?"

TUNA TIDBITS

Inspired by Episode 160: "Deep-Sea Fishing" (Season 6)

WHEN YOU'RE GOING fishing, it's not important how many fish you catch; it's the sport that counts. Needing quick cash to cover what they spent shopping, Lucy and Ethel offer to go deep-sea fishing with the boys, betting them $150 that they can land a bigger catch. In order to rig the odds, both Lucy and Ethel and Fred and Ricky buy hundred-pound tunas. To try and hide their deception from each other, the pairs end up dragging the two fish back and forth to each other's bathtubs. If you happen to find yourself with an excess of seafood on your hands, try this recipe for tuna tidbits served up in dainty lettuce cups.

MAKES 8 SERVINGS

8 small butter lettuce leaves	1 teaspoon chopped parsley
2 cans (5 ounces) tuna in water, drained	1 teaspoon lemon juice
½ cup mayonnaise	½ teaspoon onion powder
3 tablespoons celery, minced	¼ teaspoon salt
3 teaspoons pickle relish	¼ teaspoon freshly ground black pepper

- Wash and dry the lettuce leaves. Set aside.
- In a medium bowl, stir together the tuna, mayonnaise, celery, relish, parsley, lemon juice, and onion powder. Season with salt and pepper.
- Add a spoonful of tuna into each lettuce leaf, to serve.

WATERCRESS SANDWICHES

Featured in Episode 159: "Off to Florida" (Season 6)

◇◇

YOU NEVER WANT to find yourself on a road trip with a possible serial mur-
derer. Nor do you want to find yourself on the road without a good lunch. Lucy
and Ethel are to take the train down to Florida to meet up with Ricky, Fred, and
Little Ricky, who are on a fishing trip—only Lucy can't find the train tickets. The
women decide the best solution is to share a ride with a certain Mrs. Grundy,
who's driving down that way. As Mrs. Grundy naps, Lucy and Ethel hear on the
radio that a famous hatchet murderess has escaped from prison and is heading south in a cream-colored convertible coupe—the very car model in which
they happen to be hitching a ride. Through all the hubbub, the girls realize they
haven't eaten and Mrs. Grundy offers them some of her watercress sandwiches.
While Lucy thinks they taste like buttered grass, this recipe elevates the tea
sandwich and takes watercress to the next level with the addition of a light crab
salad, perfect for when you're on the run.

FOR THE CRAB SALAD
8 ounces crabmeat, drained
1 celery rib, minced
¼ cup mayonnaise
½ teaspoon yellow mustard
½ teaspoon lemon juice
½ teaspoon garlic salt
¼ teaspoon paprika

½ teaspoon freshly ground black pepper

FOR THE SANDWICHES
3 tablespoons unsalted butter, at room temperature
8 slices thin white bread
1 bunch fresh watercress, washed and dried

- In a medium bowl, stir together the crabmeat, celery, mayonnaise, yellow mustard, lemon juice, garlic salt, paprika, and pepper.
- Spread the butter onto the bread.
- Spread a layer of crab salad onto four of the buttered bread slices. Top with watercress. Place the other four slices of bread on top, to sandwich.
- Slice into triangles, to serve or pack up for your next road trip.

PART EIGHT

SPECIAL OCCASIONS

OVER THE YEARS on *I Love Lucy*, our favorite foursome celebrated anniversaries, birthdays, and the biggest festive event of all: the birth of Little Ricky. Inspired by such heartwarming scenes, this chapter highlights food for life's big events.

Take, for instance, the pregnancy-themed episodes. In one, Ricky starts to feel neglected because of all the attention on Lucy and the baby, so Fred lifts his spirits by throwing him a "daddy shower"/stag party to which every guest brings a bottle of beer. The recipe for Daddy Shower Beer Punch on page 174 elevates everyday beer to a refreshment that's sure to please a whole crowd.

In the episode "Sentimental Anniversary," Lucy and Ricky are looking forward to a quiet dinner at home on their special day, but Fred and Ethel throw them a surprise party instead. While Lucy and Ricky hide out in the closet, the Mertzes arrive with a cake and champagne. The Sentimental Anniversary Cake on page 164 is a classic white cake with a fluffy frosting that is perfect for any special occasion.

When you have something exciting to celebrate, just peruse this chapter to impress your friends with a treat brought to you by one of Lucy's big events!

SENTIMENTAL ANNIVERSARY CAKE

Featured in Episode 82: "Sentimental Anniversary" (Season 3)

EVEN THOUGH THE Ricardos would rather celebrate their anniversary alone, Fred and Ethel thoughtfully go to the trouble of throwing them a surprise party. To try and keep their small celebration private, Lucy and Ricky hide in the coat closet for some alone time before sneaking out and enjoying the festivity held in their honor. This classic 1950s silver cake is the ultimate party dessert. Fluffy and sweet, it's a beautiful way to celebrate, whether among two lovebirds or to feed a whole crowd.

MAKES 8 TO 10 SERVINGS

FOR THE CAKE

2½ cups sifted cake flour, plus more as needed for the pans

3 teaspoons baking powder

½ teaspoon salt

¾ cup (1½ sticks) unsalted butter, at room temperature, plus more as needed for the pans

1½ cups granulated sugar

1 cup whole milk

1 teaspoon almond extract

1 teaspoon vanilla

6 large egg whites

FOR THE FROSTING

3 cups confectioners' sugar

1 cup (2 sticks) unsalted butter, at room temperature

1 teaspoon vanilla

⅛ teaspoon salt

2 to 3 tablespoons whole milk, as needed

• Preheat the oven to 350°F. Grease two 8-inch-round cake pans with butter and line pans with parchment paper, then grease the parchment.

• In a large bowl, whisk together the cake flour, baking powder, and salt.

• In the bowl of an electric mixer, cream the butter and sugar.

• Whisk together the milk, almond extract, and vanilla in a glass measuring cup. With the mixer on low speed, alternate adding the wet ingredients with the dry ingredients to the creamed butter, until just incorporated.

- In a separate large bowl with clean beaters, whip the egg whites using an electric mixer until stiff. Fold them into the batter by hand using a spatula.
- Pour the batter into prepped pans. Bake for 25 minutes, or until an inserted toothpick comes out clean. Let cool 10 to 15 minutes, until cakes are cool enough to handle, then invert them onto wire racks to cool completely.
- In the bowl of an electric mixer, beat the confectioners' sugar and butter until very fluffy.
- Stir in the vanilla and salt. Add milk as needed to get a smooth frosting, then frost the cake.
- Hopefully you have a chance to enjoy the first two slices with just your honey, before dividing it up for a party of well-meaning pals.

ETHEL'S BIRTHDAY BERRY TRIFLE

Inspired by Episode 106: "Ethel's Birthday" (Season 4)

◇◇

IT'S ETHEL'S BIRTHDAY and over the years Fred hasn't exactly celebrated to her liking. After gifting her a none-too-attractive stole, and having her cook her own birthday dinner, this is the year Fred wants to make up for his past mistakes. He enlists Lucy to find the perfect present, and she comes up with brightly colored hostess pants that Ethel likens to bizarre checkerboard britches. After finding out it was Lucy who was responsible for the strange gift, Ethel gets into a huge (though temporary) fight with her. Poor Ethel can't catch a break in terms of gifts, but there's one thing she'll never say no to, and that's dessert. This retro berry trifle is as delicious as it is beautiful—a birthday treat you can't go wrong with.

MAKES 8 TO 10 SERVINGS

1 pint blueberries	1½ cups whole milk
1 pint strawberries	2 cups heavy whipping cream
1 pint raspberries	½ cup confectioners' sugar
2 tablespoons lemon juice	¼ teaspoon salt
2 tablespoons granulated sugar	1 (12 ounces) pound cake, cubed
1 box (5 ounces) instant vanilla pudding	Mint leaves, for garnish

• In a medium bowl, toss the blueberries, strawberries, and raspberries with lemon juice and sugar. Set aside.

• In a separate medium bowl, beat together pudding mix and milk. Set aside in the refrigerator.

• In the bowl of an electric mixer fitted with the whisk attachment, whip the heavy whipping cream, confectioners' sugar, and salt, until soft peaks form. Reserve 1 cup of whipped cream.

• Fold the vanilla pudding into the rest of the whipped cream mixture.

• In a trifle bowl, alternate layers of cake, cream, and fruit. Repeat the layering, then top the final layer with the reserved whipped cream. Garnish with mint leaves.

• Chill in refrigerator until ready to serve. This dessert is better than any gift you can buy!

LUCY:
"Ricky Ricardo, I'm surprised at you! It's not nice to ask a woman's age."

ETHEL:
"Thanks Lucy."

LUCY:
"Besides, it's none of your business if Ethel is 53."

ETHEL:
"I am not! I'm only— oh no you don't."

LUCY:
"Ha ha! Darn it! It almost worked."

ETHEL:
"You think you're so smart. I'll never tell you my age."

CHRISTMAS CRANBERRY SALAD

Inspired by Episode 180, "The I Love Lucy Christmas Show" (Season 6)

◇◇◇

CHRISTMAS IS A time of year when you can reflect on years past and look forward to the future. In this special, the gang trims the Christmas tree and waits for Santa as they take a look back at episodes that were particularly meaningful. Featuring clips from "Lucy Is Enceinte," "Lucy's Show Biz Swan Song," and "Lucy Goes to the Hospital," the reflection of the show's famed pregnancy episodes was especially touching. This retro cranberry gelatin salad would be ideal for any tree-trimming party. Serve it to your friends and family while looking back at significant moments in your life.

MAKES 12 SERVINGS

1 box (6 ounces) cherry gelatin	1 cup whole cranberry sauce
1½ cups boiling water	1 cup canned mandarin oranges, drained
2 cups cold lemon-lime soda	

• In a bowl stir together the cherry gelatin and boiling water, stirring until the gelatin has dissolved. Stir in the lemon-lime soda. Refrigerate for 1½ hours until slightly thickened.

• Fold in the cranberry sauce and oranges. Pour into a 6-cup ring-mold, greased with nonstick spray. Cover and refrigerate overnight.

• Unmold, and slice to serve. Maybe leave a little plate of this treat out for Santa; he'd surely appreciate it!

Lucy was TV's first expectant mother. The episode "Lucy Is Enceinte" was scandalous at the time; the script famously had to dance around saying the word "pregnant," a term CBS deemed too vulgar for air, hence the French word for pregnancy in the episode title.

Lucy's Pregnancy Cravings

The episode "Lucy Is Enceinte" reveals to the world—and Ricky—that Lucy is expecting, and the laugh-filled, pregnancy-themed episodes that follow give viewers an inside look into the life of an expectant woman.

For many, pregnancy cravings are very real! The combinations of sweet and sour or spicy and bitter are unappetizing to some, but irresistible to this particular *infanticipating* mama. Some foods that tickle Lucy's taste buds include pickles, fruit, olives, and creamy desserts—sometimes all mixed up together.

In the episode "Lucy Hires an English Tutor," Ricky returns to the apartment with a prized find—a papaya juice milkshake and a pickle. Watching Lucy gleefully dip the sour dill into the fruity blend almost makes you want to try it . . . almost.

When Ricky starts feeling his own phantom pangs in "Ricky Has Labor Pains," Lucy's enthusiasm rubs off on him. Ricky succumbs to the cravings, heartily digging in to arguably the worst of her urges: pistachio ice cream topped with hot fudge and sardines.

Try re-creating these foods at your own risk, if you can stomach it!

DADDY SHOWER
BEER PUNCH

Inspired by Episode 54: "Ricky Has Labor Pains" (Season 2)

◇◇

WITH ALL THE attention centered on Lucy and the impending arrival of their bundle of joy, Ricky's feeling neglected. Like any best friend would do, Fred throws him a manly baby shower . . . or is it a stag party? Here the gifts are full of cheer—all bottles of beer! This beer-based punch has a sweet and fruity kick and is the perfect way to toast to your soon-to-be expanded family.

MAKES 4 SERVINGS

3 cups cold pineapple juice
2 cups cold lemon-lime soda
5 tablespoons freshly squeezed lime juice

1 bottle (16 ounces) beer
Ice, for serving

• In a large pitcher, stir together the pineapple juice, lemon-lime soda, and lime juice.
• Pour in the beer, and stir again.
• Serve over glasses filled with ice. This hopsy punch is the best way to say "cheers" to fatherhood.

DOCTOR:

"Think of all your symptoms. You say you have morning sickness, right? Pains in the stomach? Dizziness? Don't you see Ricky, they're exactly like the symptoms your wife has been having lately."

RICKY:

"Oh, no. Come on! What, are you going to tell me, that *I'm* gonna have a baby?!"

SUPER ICEBOX CAKE

Inspired by Episode 166: "Lucy and Superman" (Season 6)

◇◇

WHEN LUCY FINDS out that Superman actor George Reeves is in town, she promises Little Ricky that the superhero will show up to his birthday party, even though Ricky warns her: you shouldn't "cross your bridges before they're hatched," or "burn your chickens behind you." In other words: Never make a promise you can't keep! Lucy decides to dress up as Superman to play the part herself. Only instead of appearing outside of the window as planned, she gets stuck out on the building ledge. Luckily, the real Superman swoops in and saves the day—and Lucy from the pigeon perch she's been sitting on. You'd think the kids would notice the difference between the Man of Steel and a redheaded imposter, but Lucy hopes they're so logy with ice cream and cake, they won't realize it. This retro icebox cake happens to taste like a combination of both cake and ice cream, giving you the best of both worlds in one bite!

GEORGE REEVES:

"Do you mean to say that you've been married to her for fifteen years?... And they call *me* Superman!"

MAKES 10 SERVINGS

3½ cups heavy whipping cream	50 chocolate sandwich cookies
1½ cups confectioners' sugar	¼ cup chocolate syrup
1 teaspoon vanilla	1 cup crushed sandwich cookies, for decoration
¼ teaspoon salt	

• In the bowl of an electric mixer fitted with the whisk attachment, beat the heavy whipping cream, confectioners' sugar, vanilla, and salt, until stiff peaks form.
• In a 13- x 9-inch baking pan, spread a layer of the whipped cream mixture on the bottom of the pan.
• Top with a layer of sandwich cookies (about half). Spread a layer of whipped cream, then another layer of cookies. Finish with a layer of whipped cream.
• Refrigerate overnight.
• Drizzle with chocolate syrup and sprinkle the top with chocolate crumbs.
• Slice to serve. With this easy recipe, you should even have extra time to plan a spectacle for pint-sized party guests as grand as Superman himself!

Acknowledgments

TO MY FAMILY: To Kyle, Tyler, and Mason, thank you for eating never-ending plates of my food, and for everything, always. To Gram, Alice Kawakami, Mark and Chia-Ling Kawakami, Lori Okada and Pi Sao, Chad Okada and Shirley Jou, Tracey Fujikawa, Becky and Joel Okada, Alma and Daniel Fujikawa, Aidan, Gwen, Kolten, and Penelope, thank you for all the support.

To the taste-testers: To Chrissy Dinh, Sarah Kuhn, and Mel Caylo, for dropping everything to help me whenever I need it. To Chrys Hasegawa, Mary Yogi, Jeff Chen, Cheryl deCarvalho, and Liza Palmer, for always cheering me on. To the Pool Group who let me leave food on their doorsteps: Lisa Arellano, Luz and Isabela Rodriguez, Caroline Sanjume, Pam Swart, and Sara Webster. To Robb Pearlman, thanks for always believing in me. To Cindy Sipala, thank you for being with me every step of the way.

Growing up in Los Angeles I was raised on KTLA's *I Love Lucy* reruns. I'd watch them over and over, inevitably memorizing lines and scenes. Even though Lucy was a housewife in New York and the show took place long before I was born, I could somehow identify with the zany, loveable redhead. To Lucille Ball, thank you for all the wonderful inspiration and for making a show that will always bring me joy and laughter when I need it.

This book is for my two boys, who always have to wait for the food to be photographed before they eat.

INDEX